THE JAGUAR SCRAPBOOK

THE **JAGUAR** SCRAPBOOK

Philip Porter

Foulis

Haynes

Other books of interest to Jaguar enthusiasts from the same publisher:
Jaguar E-type – the definitive history by Philip Porter (F580)
Jaguar Project XJ40 – the inside story of the new XJ6 by Philip Porter (F597)
Jaguar – the complete illustrated history 2nd ed. by Philip Porter (F750)
Jaguar Saloon Cars 2nd Ed. by Paul Skilleter (F596)
Jaguar Sports Cars by Paul Skilleter (F166)
Jaguar Sports Racing & Works Competition Cars to 1953 by Andrew Whyte (F277)
Jaguar Sports Racing & Works Competition Cars from 1954 by Andrew Whyte (F319)
Jaguar – World Champions! by Andrew Whyte (F670)
Jaguar XJR Group C & GTP Cars by Ian Bamsey (F752)
Jaguar SS90 & SS100 Super Profile by Andrew Whyte (F372)
Jaguar XK120 & 140 Super Profile by Philip Porter (F573)
Jaguar D-type & XKSS Super Profile by Andrew Whyte (F371)
Jaguar Mk2 Saloons Super Profile by Paul Skilleter (F307)
Jaguar E-type Super Profile by Andrew Whyte (F370)
Jaguar – a tradition of sports cars by Bernard Viart & Michael Cognet (F456)
The Jaguar XK by Chris Harvey (P057)
E-type: end of an era by Chris Harvey (P116)

A **Foulis** Motoring Book

First published 1989
© Philip Porter 1989

Published by:
Haynes Publishing Group
Sparkford, Near Yeovil, Somerset BA22 7JJ

Haynes Publications Inc.
861 Lawrence Drive, Newbury Park, California 91320,
USA

British Library Cataloguing in Publication Data
Porter, Philip
  Jaguar scrapbook
  1. Jaguar cars
  I. Title
  629.2'222

  ISBN .i. 0-85429-744-8

Library of Congress catalog card number 89-84709

Editor: Mansur Darlington
Page Design/Layout: Mike King
Printed in England by: J. H. Haynes & Co. Ltd

Contents

Pure . . .

Introduction

I have written something like eight books on the subject of Jaguars in the last five years! They have ranged from lightweights to heavyweights, from general histories to those on single models. My medical advisers do, however, feel that, at last, I am beginning to respond to treatment!

Like everything in life, there is always more to things than meets the eye. Writing motoring books is no exception, and for every treat – say driving a D-type – there is much midnight oil to be burned. To offset the inevitable drudgery, one very real pleasure I have had is meeting so many of the people who played a part in the charismatic Jaguar story. I have interviewed perhaps 200 Jaguar men and women in the last few years, sometimes talking specifically in relation to a particular model, sometimes tracing their career – often we have digressed!

I particularly enjoy the human side of motor car manufacture and motor sport. I love the anecdotes, the personal reminiscences, the insights, the humour and the irony. This book is an attempt to share those aspects of the Jaguar story in a series of quotes running from mere snippets to more lengthy chats.

In my quest for Jaguar information I have been given, lent or allowed to view much fascinating paperwork and illustrative material over the period, some of this, too, can be shared here.

I hope I am right in saying that it is the interesting little facts and fragments that come to light from time to time, that fellow enthusiasts find fascinating. Did you know, for instance, that there was to be an XK150 in 1950? Knowing that there was, is hardly going to change your life, but surely it is all part of the fun.

This book intended to be a fun Jaguar book, and by definition a miscellany cannot have any great structure to it. We have arranged items loosely in decades, but the idea is that the reader can work from cover to cover, or dip in here and there, as he chooses.

Above all, I hope you will be able to share a little of the fun I have had meeting a marvellous crowd of people who have contributed in all manner of ways to creating the cars and legend that we all revere.

Quite clearly such a book would not be possible without the help and enthusiasm of all the victims of my dictaphone, and those who have lent or given me so much material. It *is* invidious to single out people, but I should like to thank Arnold Bolton, Jose Freedman and Roger Clinkscales at Jaguar, George Thomson for his artwork especially created for the book, and the late Bill Heynes for giving me much fascinating paperwork. I would like to express my gratitude to Jaguar Cars plc and Stirling Moss for permission to reproduce various items. Finally, to every one of those quoted and who has contributed material, my very sincere thanks.

On the publishing side, I would like to give due credit to Rod Grainger, of Haynes/Foulis for having the imagination to understand my rather different concept, to say nothing of the nerve to go ahead with it. I would particularly like to thank Mansur Darlington for his sterling work and help in bringing it to fruition.

Philip Porter
Knighton-on-Teme,
Worcs.

. . . Bliss

PRE-WAR

MRS CONSTANCE TEATHER, who joined the young Swallow Company in 1928 as Miss Connie Dickson.

'I left school when I was about 16^1/$_2$ and worked for a short time for a firm called the Blackpool Rubber Company. I lived at Fleetwood, which was a little fishing town 10 miles away, and Blackpool was the big town in which to find work. This company sold tyres but went out of business after about nine months.

'After that I used to go to the library in Blackpool to look at the Situations Vacant, and found an advertisement for the Swallow Coachbuilding Company. So I went to see them and I think I must have been a day after everybody else. I got there on the Monday and all the crowd of young ladies who'd been answering the advertisement had been on Saturday morning – everybody worked Saturday morning then.

'That was the first time I met Alice Fenton. After waiting a little while, I was shown into Mr Lyons's office and he gave me a test of shorthand, which I had to type up as a letter, and percentages and decimals. Then we talked about wages, and I was offered five shillings a week.

'I said, "Oh no, I can't come for five shillings a week because it costs more than that for me to come on the train from Fleetwood". So then he suggested 10 shillings a week and I agreed, because I was very anxious to work.

I asked Connie if she had any idea of why she had been chosen in preference to all the others.

'Alice told me later, when I got to know her well, that at least I didn't smell of scent and I could do the sums. I think he was very good at finding somebody who was down to earth and not too fancy. I was more-or-less just a schoolgirl. That would have been April 1928.

'I used to stay for lunch and had sandwiches because I couldn't go home. Alice Fenton lived on the south shore and the Swallow Coach-building Company was on the north shore, and we grew very friendly. I think she found me very funny! We did enjoy each other's company very much and I used to walk with her along the promenade at lunchtime and we got to know each other better as the summer went by.

'The firm was then in the Cocker Street premises, which are still there and not very different – slightly altered inside. It was quite modern as a factory. Of course they had been in very poor premises earlier; Alice Fenton and Harry Teather had both worked in them. I think Alice joined in 1926 and Harry had joined in '23, so he was a long-time employee in '28!

'There was a factory sliding door, with a little wicket gate cut into it, and inside on the left was the office. This was very home-built, being made of a plywood bottom and glass top, with a little window that lifted for callers to enquire. Alice sat there in the Enquiry Office. She was the junior then and another woman, Miss Atkinson, who was mature – she seemed very old to me, she was 35ish and very staid – was Mr Lyons's secretary. Also there was the Secretary of the company, all downstairs in the office.

'Then Mr Lyons and Mr Walmsley shared an inner sanctum, but they had just one telephone which was on a little shelf on the wall and when Mr Lyons had to speak on the telephone, he came out of his office and talked there in the General Office. I was interviewed in Mr Lyons's office but when I arrived the next Monday morning to start, I was shown up into the attic, which was the stores.

'It was up a flight of stairs on to the first storey. That was the big floor that was really the only workshop. Downstairs where the office was, there was a big new paintshop where the cars were brought down and kept very clean. At great expense they'd covered the walls and ceiling in cotton sheeting, so that no dust would penetrate, and they could get a very good coachbuilt finish. Cars were just starting in production then.

'When you'd walked up these rickety stairs, you had to traverse the whole of the work floor and then at the other end – with an anvil at the bottom for the blacksmith – there was another set of rickety stairs. You went down four steps into a storeroom, which was where the sidecars were stored and painted, and up four steps to the stores. In the corner of the stores, was a little office with a skylight. That's where Mr Whittaker was installed, and I was his typist.

'There'd been another girl there before me, but she had left for a better job and also because she'd been asked to give out screws from the stores when the men came up with a chit for different articles. I didn't know anything about this but when they said that the men would come up and I must get what they needed from the stores, I said, "Oh no, I started as a shorthand typist. I think that's what I should be!" I also didn't know then that work was increasing all the time.

'So they said, "We'll have to send for Harry Teather". He was downstairs painting sidecars with a man called Cyril Marshall, who was a wonderful pianist who played in a danceband in the hotels in the evening. But Mr Walmsley was the rough diamond of the staff and he said, "Ooh, we can't say Cyril – that's far too sissy a name. We'll have to call you Sam". So he was always known as Sam!

'Of course I didn't know anybody and was very shy when I first arrived. I had to use a very old Oliver typewriter which I found a bit difficult, but I soon got into the work. Apparently, Mr Whittaker had been the sidecar salesman but they had been selling so well and Mr Lyons confessed that, really, he wasn't very good as a salesman – he was so good himself – and so he brought Mr Whittaker in to do the buying.

'Mr Whittaker eventually became known as the most astute buyer in the whole of the motor trade.

'Apart from advertising and sales, I think everything else was more-or-less designated upstairs to our office. I used to have to go down every morning for the post, once Mr Lyons had scanned it. We didn't do accounts, of course, that went to the secretary. We did the service queries, of which there were very few at that time because only a few cars had gone out.

'It had only been the previous year that they had had one car, I think, and Mr Henly had asked them to put it outside Olympia to see what the reaction was. And, of course, lots of people were very interested in it. So in the summer of 1928 they had just got one or two orders from different agents and progress was very slow at that time. However, most of our business in that office was spares for sidecars.

'One of Harry's jobs as a young boy, before he was promoted to the paintshop, had been to make crates to send the sidecars away in. Also we had to have different joints to attach to different types of motorbike – like BSA, Douglas and Ariel Square-Four. They all had different joints and so these had to be despatched. I had a system with a book to give instructions to Harry Teather in the stores to make the parcel up, and then it came back to me and I had to take the parcels to the post. I had a post book to see how much had been spent on postage.

'It was in that way that I got to know Harry because, when I was very laden, he asked if he could carry my parcels. That's how we got to know each other and became friends.'

I wondered how Lyons and Walmsley struck Connie in those early days.

'I was only 17 and, although they were very young, they didn't strike me as young 'cause to me they were old! Mr Lyons was married with a baby. He was always very smart with a very short-back-and-sides haircut. They were both always in Plus Fours, but that was the Prince of Wales's favourite outfit. It was very unusual, unless he was going on a special visit, that Mr Lyons came in a suit.

'Mr Walmsley was obviously more mature, and very hearty. One of the unforgettable experiences was when he said, "Has Fat made this putrid tea?" That was me, because I was as broad as I was long in those days! That was one of my duties to look after the tea.

'Mr Lyons was full of energy but I really didn't appreciate what was going on in the firm because I was stuck up in this attic. Eventually I could reply to the letters blindfold, knowing more-or-less what Mr Whittaker was going to say, unless it was some special query, and often Harry would help me or I would ask somebody in the works. Mr Whittaker always seemed to be up and down. He would probably be seeing reps downstairs. He would stand with them inside the factory somewhere.

'It was a very small company and I think they did everything by trial and error in those days. Mr Holland was there. He'd been imported from Wolverhampton as a specialist body designer and he had a board and easel near the window where he drew. Also there were two mature men, who were also body builders.

'The body builders were all raised in the middle of the room and then by the window there was one sewing machine for the trimming. Right in the corner at the bottom of the stairs where I came up to the stores was a welding machine and an anvil. That was the machine shop! Jack Bearsley was the blacksmith – he called himself a whitesmith – and he had a young boy who altered the starting handles.

'The chassis came in with the ordinary Austin Seven starting handle but because they fitted a newly designed radiator cowl, they needed far more length. So it was this poor youngster's job to saw away with a hacksaw and then put a distance piece between and Jack used to weld them.

'Harry Gill was also there. He was in charge of fitting the body to the chassis. In the summer of 1928 they got the order for 500 from Henlys and they were dismayed to find that Austin sent a whole batch of cars. They all arrived at Blackpool station and, of course, the railway company were livid. They wanted the room. It was summer and everywhere was chock-a-block. I remember these chassis being towed to the works and there were chassis everywhere, surrounding the factory.

'Apart from the office and paintshop, at the back of the works on the ground floor was a big lift and it was, apparently, the biggest in the north of England. One Sunday, that summer, Segrave had his *Miss England* and asked permission to use the lift so that it could be hoisted on to a lorry to be taken to the Lakes.

'That lift was used to take the chassis upstairs to be mounted, and then they all had to come downstairs to be painted. They must have been painted after they were mounted, which was the reverse of what happened in Coventry. The Marsh brothers were in charge of the workshop and they had come from Wolverhampton too. Everybody was very friendly and always making jokes.

'It was a very happy company to work for, I think, because we were all young. It was traditional that on Friday afternoon people would be wanting their wages and work till half past five. But Mr Lyons wouldn't have gone to the bank for them, he'd be far too busy! So they all had to wait till the next day for their wages, and then they were grumbling.

'Mr Lyons was very ambitious and he must have taken some risks, but when he received the big order from Henlys that must have been very profitable. He was just determined that they would fulfil it.'

Did Lyons – I asked Mrs Teather – ever roll up his sleeves and get stuck in himself?

'No. Not that I remember. He wasn't a practical man. It was Mr Holland who transcribed his thoughts on to the board. Then Mr Holland would do a mock-up and we'd have small models in plasticine sometimes. Then he'd see if it looked right.

' "No, not low enough, Holland, Not low enough."

'It obviously couldn't be made any lower. The Austin Seven Swallow had footwells so that it would not be too high and look sporty. Mr Lyons once said that without Cyril Holland transcribing his ideas, he could not have achieved what he wanted to do.

'I think he was only looking for a business to go into. He'd tried music and various things with his father before he went into the motor trade. Both he and Mr Walmsley were very keen on the motor trade and they met at the Blackpool races which operated on Blackpool Sands.

'Mr Lyons was just very keen to go into business, whereas Mr Walmsley was more-or-less independent, and just wanted a nice quiet life. It was only for something to do that he started it. He never had the same urgency to get on and get things done. He was more interested in designing and I think he would have designed other things if the pressure on the cars hadn't been so great.

'Mr Lyons was always very formal even in those days and called everybody by their surnames. I was Miss Dickson even in his later years. That was the way they were in the twenties.

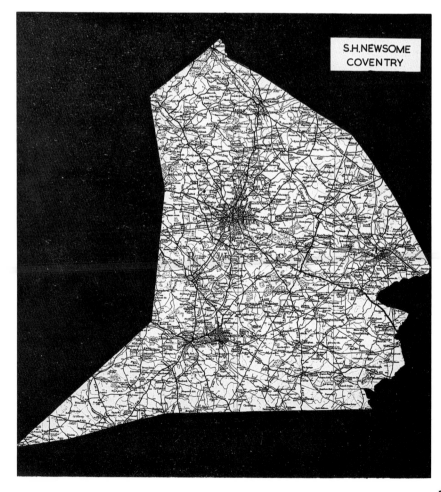

S.H. NEWSOME
COVENTRY

This is how Newsome's illustrated 'their' Jaguar territory. (Jaguar Cars).

'It was a great shock to me when the notice went up on the board to say that they had decided to move to Coventry. Alice confided to me that Mr Lyons had requested her to ask her parents if she could come to Coventry. At that time a job was available in the office at the Opera House and her family was quite theatrical and very musical. She was very torn between the two, and did apply and go for an interview. She thought that was just as exciting as the motor industry.

'Anyway she confided in me that she was going to Coventry and she said, "Come on young Con, you come. Ask yer dad if you can come. Go and see Mr Lyons."

'So I went to see Mr Lyons and asked if I could come to Coventry.

' "Come to Coventry? How old are you? Seventeen! Have you asked your parents?"

'When I said that I hadn't he suggested I had better go and find another job, so I did. There happened to be a job in Fleetwood but I was very sorry to leave. That was about the end of October. They went down to Coventry in different groups. We'd no idea what Coventry was like or anything about it. On the clock there was a list of landladies that the boys could apply to for lodgings. You had to put your name down if you were going. Harry said he wasn't going 'cause he earned 30 shillings a week and what was the good of him going and not being able to afford any digs.

'Gradually the body builders went and the trimmers went. They had to take on more labour in Coventry and they had to get a Works Manager in Coventry because Mr Lyons couldn't be in two places at once. He was called Mr Etches. I can't remember when the painters left but Alice was due to go on 22 October and that was after the Motor Show.

'Mr Lyons and Mr Walmsley took Alice down, and I think Harry went about the same time. I'd left the week before and Harry was packing up the parts and putting the contents into great packing cases in the stores when Mr Lyons had come and offered him a rise to about three pounds ten, so that he could afford to live. So he agreed to go down.

'I went to the Boston Deep Sea Fishing Co. but that was a great change and I didn't like it very much. After a fortnight, on the Saturday morning there was a telegram to say, "If interested Coventry call Bispham Road at 3pm Sunday".

'My mother was away, so my sister Margaret and I went on the tram to Bispham Road and found Mr Lyons's bungalow. Mrs Lyons opened the door and she was carrying Pat on her arm. She chatted to us and Mr Lyons came in and said that Miss Fenton was fed-up and lonely with nobody to talk to, and all the work was piling up, and Mr Whittaker had no time to do it, and he hadn't found anybody else either, and would I want to go down.

'I said yes, and he wanted to know if I'd asked my father. But I knew he would let me come if I wanted to as long as I was with Alice. She was more mature and had more common sense than I had. She was very obviously ambitious, although she didn't look sophisticated and still had a long plait. Mr Lyons had said, the day before she was due to go, that she ought to put her hair up to look more sophisticated for Coventry!

'My father said I could go. He thought I would be back in a month. Mr Lyons and Mr Walmsley had brought Alice back up for the weekend, because both their wives were still in Blackpool. So he arranged for me to meet him at Talbot Road Station at nine o'clock. He picked me up and we went to Alice's house, and then on to Coventry. I had no idea where Coventry even was and he says, "Do you know anything about Coventry?" to make conversation.

'I enjoyed the drive very much indeed. I think we were in Mr Walmsley's Alvis, and I have the mascot on my mantelpiece because he

'Lyons spent most of his time thinking about Jaguar, even when people were talking about something else. He was a very conservative man, but a fast driver.

ALAN NEWSOME
Company Solicitor

'There was extraordinary loyalty to the company and to Lyons. Jaguar prestige was so great that it was something to be associated with the company.'

ALAN NEWSOME
Company solicitor

According to a Mr T. Carlisle of Bramhall, Cheshire some of the first Swallow sidecar bodies were made in a barnlike building adjacent to the Bamford Arms public house on Buxton Road, Heaviley, Stockport, Cheshire.

gave it to Harry to look after for him later on. He was a very quick driver, Mr Lyons.

'Alice and I shared a room in our digs, which were in Holmesdale Road near the Courtaulds factory. My Lyons and Mr Walmsley were in St. Paul's Road. We thought Courtaulds was fabulous – this great big factory full of light. We weren't used to industry at all. We used to walk past it, along Holbrook Lane to Swallow Road, not that it was called that then. It was just a muddy patch.

'At Blackpool, Mr Lyons had said, "How much wage do you want to come down to Coventry? Do you know how much you'll need?"

'I'd no idea. I just gave my money to my mother, so I replied that I would need 35 shillings. I said that because Miss Atkinson earned 35 shillings. I thought that was a most fabulous wage.

'The digs cost a pound a week. The first week it rained every day and it was such a muddy road, I spent 15 shillings on a pair of Wellingtons. So I had no money till the next week!

'Mr Whittaker was seeing reps all day long because the word had got around that this new place was starting up. It was slump time so everyone came to try and get some business.

'The offices were built more-or-less the same but on a larger scale at Coventry. It was a disused mine factory, built in the First World War by Lloyd George's Government. The little windows were slits across so that if there was any bomb blast it wouldn't affect anything. So we had very little sunshine or daylight. When I first went the walls were all wringing wet because it had not been occupied for a long time and everywhere was very damp.

'You went in the factory door, the same as you did at Blackpool, and the office was still on the left, but the dimensions were bigger. I occupied the enquiry office, because I started being the enquiry girl, and then there was Mr Whittaker's office, which he never seemed to be in. I think he never seemed to be in there, except to dictate letters, because he liked having his ear cocked at the enquiry office to see who was coming to see him, at the same time talking to a rep in the corner. They used to smoke incessantly, and you couldn't see across the office for smoke.

'I was answering the telephone and dealing with enquiries, and sending spare parts orders out to Harry Teather, and answering as many service query letters as I could. When material was required, Harry would give me a list, or Mr Whittaker would. He always had to vet what Harry ordered. Then in my spare time, if any, I would check the orders against the material received and check the price. If everything was OK, it could be passed to Accounts for payment. The only thing was we ordered panels, at that time, in sets – nearside bonnet panel, offside bonnet panel; nearside door panel, offside door panel.

'I'd not a clue what offside and nearside were, and what wings were, and how to make them up into sets!

'After some time, we found that we were getting charged 10 shillings for a crate. All these crates had been thrown outside in the rain, 'cause everybody was very busy, and Harry had the job of packing all the crates and labelling them so that they could be returned to get the money back.

'After Mr Whittaker's office, there was the accounts office, and then Alice's sales office – she was the sales department. Next came Mr Lyon's office, and then an empty office which was supposed to be for people waiting for cars, or reps. There was a passage beyond and then the stores. The stores were just being built – there were joiners up in the roof and building trestles around all the materials. All the material that Harry had stored in the boxes had been tipped upside down and just parked on the floor. So he had the job of sorting it all out again and making a list for stock purposes.

'When we arrived, he met us with the news that the electricity cable had been stolen, so there were no lights, and Mr Lyons was in a real huff then. He wanted to know how it could have happened. It was bitterly cold because it was November. I came down the day after Remembrance Sunday.

'Mr Lyons ordered some braziers, like they had on the road, so that the men could work, but the doors had to be perpetually open to let the smoke out!

'They worked for a long time with just braziers, and we had paraffin stoves. He ordered a stove to be beside each stool. At first we sat on orange boxes with benches covered in brown lino for your typewriter.

'Mr Whittaker would be talking to reps all day long and then when it got quiet and the phone stopped at half past five, we would do some letters. "This must go and that must go. We ought to do this, and this man will be irate if he doesn't get a reply". We used to go on till eight and nine doing the important letters.

'Mr Lyons would send somebody in a car – there was one man particularly who had a car, which was unusual – and they would send him to the GPO to catch the nine o'clock post. Taffy Morris was one of them. He was a toolmaker in the factory and was a very nice person. We used to get hungrier and hungrier, and there were no facilities, apart from this putrid cup of tea that I made at four o'clock, and it was known that Taffy Morris had some chocolate in his toolbox. We used to go up and buy a sixpenny bar from him, and that's how we existed.

'Mr Lyons and Mr Walmsley used to walk us home when it was late and dark. They were making plans to move, but in those first few months they used to go home regularly every three weeks, and they used to ask us if we would like to go and we always said yes. That meant that we had a morning off, coming back on the Monday morning, but we more than made up for it working late. We did attempt to go to night school, Alice and I, to learn German and French, because already we were getting enquiries for sidecars and cars in foreign languages. But we always got there as the class was finishing, so we gave up in the end.'

The Prince of Romania owned an SS Jaguar 100 which he stated he preferred to his BMW 328.

CHARLES NEEDHAM, on the 1933 International Alpine Trial, the Company's first international competitive success.

'It was quite a courageous decision for a comparatively small firm, producing touring cars, to decide to enter an official trade team in the International Alpine 1933. However, "Bill" Lyons decided to have a go and as I had in the previous year won a Coupe in an Invicta car, I was asked my opinion, and I thought that at least they would finish the course and be an advertisement for the firm.

'As was usual, in those days, I drove the whole way merely taking along a friend for helping with the necessary work – clocks and refuelling, etc. His name was D. Munro who, with that exceedingly successful and keen motorist Humphrey Symons driving the second car and Miss Margaret Allen, now Mrs Jennings, driving the third car, made up the team.

'We were particularly successful and we were able to win the team prize. If the car was not fast, it was at least reasonably reliable, with a maximum speed of 78 mph, but it had a snag of slightly overheating, which was a common fault in those days, and the steering was inclined to stiffen up on full lock and require frequent greasing.

'This, of course, can mean a loss of a second or two on every hairpin bend but in spite of that, owing to the light weight of the car, the general all-round performance was much better than people expected.

'I was rather amused a little later when I used one of these for my own journeys in England, to overhear two undergraduates in Oxford walking past, saying one to the other, "what a nice sweet smell there is around here". The reason being, of course, that they were very good smart looking cars and therefore had all sorts of rude names given to them by the new generation.

'However, those fellows were hardly likely to know that this actual car had done a marvellous job of work and had put up a better performance than many famous makes in that very tough event and, believe me, it was darned hard work. If I remember rightly there were about 135 starters.

'The next year, 1934, the firm decided again to put us in, but this time the competition had speeded up a bit and once again it was obvious we could not win a Coupe. Also the cars were rather stiff and not well run in, and practically brand new when we left for France. I decided early on that they would probably run too hot and quietly formulated the plan to use, whenever possible, 25 per cent Benzole mixture, which I took around with me and refilled or ordered the night before. I also had no practice in the Alps deliberately, but did as much running in as possible and this meant that I was the only car to go through without any distortion of the aluminium cylinder head.

'The second car was driven by A.G. Douglas-Clease and the third by S. Light. Owing to overheating, we were beaten by Clemente-Talbot, which incidentally, was a very expensive and racing set-up using modified Brooklands and Le Mans cars. They took the first team prize and we took the second team prize, with silver plaques. It was obvious from this point onwards that more power and less weight would give a definite win and from this time the 100 mph spartan SS Sports was evolved, which T.H. Wisdom later ran, and I think I am correct in saying he won the first Coupe for S.S. cars.

'These were the first successful International events which the old firm achieved under extreme difficulties and I think was very creditable, looking back, that no single car failed to finish and they did not leave the road, despite some very fast driving down hill. The roads were far more difficult then than now, being narrow and uneven, with dust and ruts, and always macadam once off the main road in the valley. Passing was very tricky and petrol stations were few and far between. All corners were bare of safety walls and actually were designed for Alpine troop movements with mule transport.'

CHARLES NEEDHAM

Bertie Henley seen in later years. It was his order for 500 Swallow-bodied Austins that forced Swallow into serious mass-production.

S.H. NEWSOME, on Old Number 8

Sammy Newsome takes the 'factory' 100 up Shelsley Walsh hill climb in September 1937 recording times of 45.92 and 45.52 seconds. (Midland Automobile Club Archive)

'The origin of the special $3\frac{1}{2}$-litre SS100 is rather interesting. This was originally a $2\frac{1}{2}$-litre SS100 of a completely standard specification which I bought for the purpose of rallies, etc., having decided to give up racing after several years of participation at Le Mans, etc., on various other makes.

'I had tried, without success, to persuade Mr Lyons (as he then was) to take an interest in speed events, but he was somewhat reluctant at that stage. I was particularly interested in Shelsley Walsh, and eventually rather forced his hand by entering this car for the event for sports cars up to 3 litres, with the intention of running it in standard form. However, Mr. Lyons was not enthusiastic about this as he particularly wanted the first SS "100" to take part in a speed event to put up a good show, and therefore a $2\frac{1}{2}$-litre engine was prepared with such minor modifications as a higher compression and a lower axle ratio, and some special fuel supplied through A.K.W. Von der Becke. I ran the car in its standard form in the Scottish Rally and left Glasgow at 5.30 p.m. on the Thursday evening at the end of the rally, arriving at the factory around midnight. The car was then taken over by the Experimental Department and the engine and back axle were changed, in addition to sundry other minor work such as the removal of surplus equipment.

'I picked up the car at 9 am the next morning and drove it to Shelsley for practice when it behaved perfectly, and succeeded in winning its class the following day. Mr Lyons was so interested in its performance that the car was kept in this form and retained as a sprint car. I was provided with another one in its place and I drove the car with this $2\frac{1}{2}$-litre engine quite successfully in several other events.

*Under-bonnet view of the SS 100
shows that the area was well-filled on
this model. (Mrs. E. Simms)*

'The following year a prototype 3½-litre engine was fitted, with a higher compression ratio, which I drove at Shelsley in what was then the very good time of 44 seconds, or thereabouts. At this stage the car was very potent and the main problem was that weight distribution was not really suitable for this type of event, and it was quite a handful. Subsequently Wally Hassan joined the company, and the chassis layout was substantially altered, the engine being set back to a considerable extent and the body being altered to reduce weight.

'A good deal of attention was paid to the engine, and it is perfectly true that it developed a figure in the region of 170 bhp. The engine was basically standard but had rather an extraordinary compression ratio which I believe was in the neighbourhood of 12½:1 and of course it ran on dope. This car put up some remarkable performances although, of course, it was always handicapped by roadholding qualities which were naturally inferior to those of specially built racing cars.

**A MR KEY writing in the
sixties (from the Ndola Club,
N. Rhodesia) of his experiences
with his S.S.I**

*Mr Key, it seems, purchased the 1933
Motor Show S.S.I which he and his
wife then drove for two years before
being forced, by an increase in the
family, to part with it.*

'The car – a very pretty shade of
Lemon/Cream with black wings, top,
etc. – was quite one of the most
comfortable I have ever driven (and
that covers a few score!).

'It was the first car in which I
actually covered 60 miles within the
hour; the place, the Winchester-
Basingstoke-Camberley Heath road on
Armistice Sunday 1934. My wife and I
were on holiday at Sidmouth when we
received an early morning phone call
to say that her mother was not
expected to live. The S.S. answered up
magnificantly and enabled my wife to
see her mother for a short time before
she died.

'At Shelsley I did eventually succeed in getting it down to the time of 41.4 secs, and in the hands of Tommy Wisdom it lapped Brooklands at over 118 mph.

'I ran this car throughout 1938 and 1939 and again in 1946 and 1947, until a weak accelerator spring upset things in the second part of the S-bend and I had a somewhat exciting argument with the bank in practice. I did actually manage to run the car the next day, but the accident caused some dislocation of my back and I had to give up racing altogether.

'This special was certainly a very exciting car, and I think its particular interest lies in the fact that it was really the first effort of the Jaguar Company at entering speed events, which may or may not have played its part in later developments, by demonstrating the commercial potentiality of participation in competitions other than rallies.

'One interesting point was that in its later form the car had a 6½:1 axle ratio and I was able to use top gear in the earlier stretch of the hill and in the finishing straight.'

―――――

'It is perfectly true that I designed and produced a special drop head coupé on the "100" chassis in 1939, but only three were built as the war broke out just as we were about to go into production.'

18

'Its only vice, as I recall, manifested itself in sudden, and usually most inconvenient, collapses of the clutch pedal push rod; it seems the rods were not man enough to cope with the clutch return spring and, after a period of time, they would suddenly bend at right angles leaving the clutch pedal flopping on the floor. This treatment was once meted out to me half way down Piccadilly in a traffic jam; you can no doubt picture the rest. I subsequently discovered the longest length axle supplied in the old Meccano kit served as an admirable substitute and, after fitting one of these, I had no further trouble.

'During the two years that we owned it, we covered some 40,000 miles wth no trouble, other than the nuisance-value of the aforementioned clutch, and on one occasion we actually essayed the ascent of Snowdon but, needless to relate, the narrowing of the track prevented our getting very far.'

G.M. KEY

ASSEMBLY WEIGHTS.

2½ Litre.

	CWTS.	LBS.
Engine complete with oil	5	81¾
Gear Box complete with oil		106½
Frame	2	88
Front axle with brake drums	1	37¾
Rear axle with brake drums	2	25¾
Front springs		54¾
Rear Springs		60¾
Shock absorbers Front		19
" " Rear		21
Four wheels with tyres	1	74
" " without tyres		78
Radiator		57
Steering column and box		38
Prop shaft		18¼
Battery		74
Four brake drums		82½
Exhaust system		27¼
Petrol tank		23
Bumpers Front		39½
" Rear		20½

An ex-factory document showing assembly weights for various SS cars.

S.S. CHASSIS AND BODY WEIGHTS.

CHASSIS.

Chassis Components.	AIRLINE cwts.	qrs.	lbs.	SS1 Saloon cwts.	qrs.	lbs.	SS1 Tourer cwts.	qrs.	lbs.	SS11 Saloon cwts.	qrs.	lbs.	SS11 Tou cwts.	qrs.	lbs
Chassis completed for mounting. (Less components shown below)	15	2	5	15	1	5	15	1	5	11	0	13	11	0	13
Engine oil.	0	0	18	0	0	18	0	0	18	0	0	10	0	0	10
Gear Box Oil.	0	0	2¼	0	0	2¼	0	0	2¼	0	0	2¼	0	0	2
Real axle oil.	0	0	3½	0	0	3½	0	0	3½	0	0	2¼	0	0	2
Front wings	0	2	10	0	2	1	0	2	1	0	1	1	0	1	1
Rear wings.	0	0	26½	0	1	0	0	1	0	0	0	20½	0	0	20½
Complete Front bumper.	0	1	19	0	1	19	0	1	19	0	0	14	0	0	14
Complete rear bumper.	0	0	18	0	1	6½	0	1	6½	0	0	26	0	0	26
Spare wheel [illegible].	(2 Spares) 0	3	10	0	1	19	0	1	19	0	1	10¾	0	1	10¾
Radiator shell block	0	2	6	0	2	6	0	2	6	0	1	18	0	1	18
Bonnett complete with tie rods, brackets & fasteners.	0	2	1	0	1	27	0	1	27	0	1	14	0	1	14
Wing step beads.	0	0	8	0	0	8	0	0	8	0	0	6	0	0	6

'The S.S.I was in a different street. It romped past most things on the road and earned the impolite soubriquet of the "Cad's Car". But it was all good publicity!'

ERIC FINDON

S.S. CHASSIS AND BODY WEIGHTS. Cont.

	AIRLINE			SS1 SALOON			SS1 TOURER			SS11 SALOON			SS11 TOURER		
Complete set of electrical equipment.	0	3	16½	0	3	15	0	3	15	0	3	11½	0	3	11½
Kit of tools	0	1	4½	0	1	4½	0	1	4½	0	1	2½	0	1	2½
Spare wheel fixing nut. (2 nuts & distance pieces)	0	0	14	0	0	3	0	0	3	0	0	2½	0	0	2½
Spare wheel cover. (2 covers.)	0	1	14	0	0	13	0	0	13	0	0	11¾	0	0	11¾
Petrol filler knock cap	0	0	3½	0	0	2	0	0z	2	0	0	1½	0	0	1½
Chassis valances 2 front aprons	0	0	23	0	0	23	0	0	23	0	0	21	0	0	2'

Components.	AIRLINE.			SS1 SALOON.			SS1 TOURER.			SS11 SALOON.			SS11 TOURER.		
	cwts.	qrs.	lbs.	cwts.	qrs.	lbs.	cwts.	qrs.	lbs.	cwts.	qrs.	lbs.	cwts.	qrs.	lbs.
Total complete chassis weight. (less water)	20	0	7	20	0	7	20	0	7	14	2	21	14	2	21
Water in radiator & engine jacket.	0	1	12	0	1	12	0	1	12	0	1	0	0	1	0
Complete body weight	5	1	9	4	2	9	5	2	7	4	3	7			
Complete car weight. (less petrol)	27	1	0	25	3	0	25	0	0	20	2	0	19	3	0

(handwritten notes on chassis row: 20 · 3 · 22; on body weight row: 5 · 3 · 22)

1 Gal. Petrol (Ethyl) = 7 lbs 6 ozs.

It should be noted when quoting any of the above figures that no two chassis, bodies or components have exactly the same weights, but the variations are sufficiently slight as to be of no consequence for all general purposes

WEIGHT OF SS1 FRONT AXLE COMPLETE WITH BRAKE DRUMS, TRACK RODS, SHOCK ABSORBERS AND ROAD SPRINGS. = 182 lbs

THE LATE MICHAEL SEDGWICK writing to Eric Findon, formerly of the magazine *Light Car,* upon the subject of the S.S.II

'I've never driven one and the comments I've heard up to now were almost uniformly "beastly little car". The late Malcolm Henderson, of Craig & Rose, the paint people, bought one for his honeymoon in, I think, 1934, and was so disgusted with it that he refused an offer of S.S. shares when the public company was floated. When I last spoke to him (1953, I think) he was still kicking himself for an error of judgement.'

ERIC FINDON replying

'Comparing the S.S.II with contemporary light cars, I would say that, in some cases, it showed up badly on performance, but held its own in equipment and appearance. The Aero Minx could make rings round it, and so could the Triumph, on the road; but without referring back, I can't say how they compared on price. Round about 1934 I had a six-cylinder Wolseley Hornet Special with free wheel. It was the cat's pyjamas until it got up to about 70 then it started to wander all over the road. No, I think that the S.S. II sold on its looks not on its performance.'

The curtain rises on the first S.S.

An advertisement placed in the 14 February 1936 *New York Times,* by Hilton Motors who were located uptown at the Grand Concourse at 151st New York City, ran as follows.

'ANNOUNCEMENT – Thirty-three of the Sensational British Standard Swallow Sports Cars will arrive in a shipment from England. These cars are in various body types and are the latest models available. Above cars will be on display at our showroom not later than Feb. 19 and can be purchased at a considerable saving.'

It is said that they were a batch of left-over 1935 cars, including examples of the rare Drophead S.S.Is.

THE AUTOCAR.   ADVERTISEMENTS.   OCTOBER 9TH, 1931.   119

Enter

the most remarkable car of the year

IN appearance and in every way a £1,000 car but . . . the price is only £310. Lower . . faster . . smarter . . utterly unique . . its introduction signalises a remarkable advancement in automobile construction. 15 h.p., 6 cylinders, 4 speeds, silent third, flashing acceleration . . . 60, 70, 75 m.p.h. Look at its delightful lines. Does it not delight the eye? Right . . then act. Get the thrill of your life . . see and try it personally at Olympia.

The new S.S. . . . . *See it on* Stand 72

a SWALLOW production

**Manufacturers: THE SWALLOW COACHBUILDING CO.,
FOLESHILL, COVENTRY.**
London Distributors: Henlys, Devonshire House,
Piccadilly, and Henly House, Euston Road.

B17   MENTION OF "THE AUTOCAR," WHEN WRITING TO ADVERTISERS, WILL ENSURE PROMPT ATTENTION.

*Even as early as 1932, suppliers of
automotive parts were keen to share in
the Swallow limelight.*

*The firm of Parkers were one of
Swallow's very first agents, and would
later be taken over by Henlys.*

CYRIL MANN, SS Jaguar 100 owner

'Prior to, and after, the last war I
regularly competed in rather a special
3.5-litre "100" model, which was
finally sold to an American in 1952 for
2000 dollars, and exported to Buffalo.
It was not until a Brighton Speed trial
in the middle forties that it was ever
beaten by another SS, and that due to
the fact that, with a 9:1 compression
ratio, I overdid the ratio of Pool petrol
and Toluene, and the car ran way
below its usual form.

'With full standard road equipment, but with screen removed, it

achieved 106 mph in 1939, 0-50 mph in
7.4 secs, and a standing lap on the
Brooklands outer circuit at over 86
mph.

'Just after the war at the first
"proper" speed trial, at Elstree, it won
the unlimited racing class (with full
equipment) and the only unblown car
to beat it was John Bolster's Bloody
Mary.

CYRIL MANN

[On a personal note, I would be very
interested to hear from anybody who
knows the whereabouts of Mr Mann
today as he owned and rallied my
XK120 Roadster! P.P.]

PLAGIARISM OR COINCIDENCE

Jaguar were not the first to use the slogan 'Grace, Space and Pace'.

In fact, as the noted MG historian, F. Wilson McComb once pointed out, in 1935/6 the MG company used the following slogan in advertising their 1½-litre and 2-litre push-rod range:

for space for grace for pace

There was also some suggestion that the famous leaping jaguar may have been inspired by a mascot which Cecil Kimber found on his travels on the continent. On his return he had a small number of replicas cast in bronze as a Tigress mascot.

Bill Rankin told the late Michael Sedgwick in the early sixties that the Jaguar mascot came about because, when the SS Jaguar was announced, one of the accessory firms brought out a horrible mascot which looked like a 'cat shot off a fence'! Rankin asked Lyons's permission to design a better one. The result was a Rankin design stylised by Gordon-Crosby. It was, of course, merely an optional extra until 1957.

Curiously Gordon-Crosby was associated with Kimber, and according to McComb owned a Mark II 18/80 saloon which MG built specially for him. The Tigress mascot was to have been fitted to the Mark III, the road-racing version of the Mark II!

The company never believed in modesty!

A tremendous amount of creative imagination always went into the company advertisements, with whole pages not even showing a car.

28th May, 1935.

Weslake

Standard Swallow 20 H.P. O.H.V. Conversion.

Parts List.

Part No.	Name.	Material	No. off.
WH.1704	Cylinder head.	C.I.	1
WH.1745	Cylinder head gasket.	C.A.	1
WH.1747	Cylinder head studs.	3% Ni.S.	19
WH.1710	Cylinder head nuts (centre row).	3% Ni.Steel.	7
WH.1717	Inlet valve.	3% Ni.Steel	6
WH.1718	Exhaust valve.	Valkrom.	6
WH.1739	Valve spring, inner.	Spring S.	12
WH.1738	Valve spring, outer.	Spring S.	12
WH.1742	Valve spring collar.	3% Ni.S.	12
WH.1744	Valve spring bottom guide.	M.S.	12
WH.1724	Split cone.	M.S.	12 pairs
WH.1716	Valve guide.	C.I.	12
WH.1711	Rocker No. 1.	3% Ni.Chrome C.H.S.	6
WH.1712	Rocker No. 2.	3% Ni.Chrome C.H.S.	6
WH.1714	Rocker bush.	Phosphor Bronze.	12
WH.1726	Rocker shaft.	M.S. drawn tube.	1
WH.1713	Rocker bracket Nos. 1 - 5.	M.I. Casting.	5
WH.1728	Rocker bracket No. 6.	M.I. Cstg.No.WH.1713	1
WH.1719	Rocker bracket stud.	M.S.	6
WH.1727	Locking screw for rocker shaft.	M.S. hex. bar.	1
	Plug for rocker oil hole.	Brass rod 1/8" dia. by 1/8" long.	24
	Nut for rocker bracket. 3/8" B.S.F.	M.S.	6
	Plain washer for rocker bkt. 3/8"	M.S.	6
	Wick for oil hole.	Lampwick 1/8" dia.	16½"
WH.1736	Rocker separating springs.	Spring steel wire.	5
WH.1737	Rocker end spring.	Flat spring steel.	2
WH.1729	End washer, rocker shaft.	M.S.	2
	End plug, rocker shaft.	3/8"B.S.F.x ½"set screw.	1
WH.1735	Rocker cover joint.	Compressed cork.	1
WH.1734	Rocker cover.	Al. Cast.	1
WH.1720	Stud for rocker cover.	M.S.	2
	Nut for rocker cover.	5/16"B.S.F.Cap nut. N.P.	2
W.H.1746	Filler cap.	Al. Cast.	1
WH.1730	Rocker oil feed banjo union.	H.D. Brass.	1
	Fibre washers.	5/8"O.D. x 3/8" x 1/32"	5
WH.1731	Union screw for above.	M.S. hex. bar.	1
	Cu. pipe, 3/16"O.D. x 21 S.W.G.	2¾" long.	
	¼" B.S.P. union.	H.D. Brass.	2
	3/16" nipple.	H.D. Brass.	2
	¼" B.S.P. union nut.	H.D. Brass.	2
	Fibre washers.	5/8"O.D. x 3/8" x 1/32"	2
WH.1774	Distributor bracket.	C.I.	1
WH.1708	Studs for distributor bracket.	M.S.	3
	Nuts, 5/16" B.S.F.	M.S.	3
	Spring washers, 5/16"	Spring S.	3
WH.1743	Distributor extension shaft.	M.S.	1
WH.1772	Exhaust manifold.	C.I.	1
WH.1709	Studs for manifold.	M.S.	15
	Nuts 3/8" B.S.F.	Brass.	15
	Spring washers, 3/8".	Spring S.	13
	3/8" B.S.F. x 1¼" bolts.	M.S.	2
W.H.1721	Joint, centre flanges.	Cu. Asb.	1
WH.1722	Joint, Nos. 2 & 5 flanges.	Cu. Asb.	2
WH.1723	Joint, Nos. 1 & 6 flanges.	Cu. Asb.	2
WH.1748	Water uptake, front.	Al. Cast.	1
WH.1749	Water uptake, rear.	Al. Cast.	1
WH.1750	Studs for water uptake.	M.S.	7
	Nuts 5/16" B.S.F.	M.S.	2
Standard	Washers, 5/16"	M.S.	7
Standard	Rubber hose for joint, 1¼" bore.	3" long.	1 piece
Standard	Clips for joint.	Jubilee 1¼"	2
WH.1732	Joint, centre.	Vellumoid, 1/32"	1
WH.1733	Joint, ends.	Vellumoid, 1/32"	2
WH.1741	Push rod.	Drawn steel tube.	12
WH.1740	Ball end.		24
WH.1754	Tappet adjusting screw.	Steel .60 carbon.	12
WH.1753	Dynamo bracket.	M.S. Press.	1
WH.1752	Dynamo bracket stud.	M.S.	2
WH.1751	Carburetter stud.	M.S.	8
WH.1769	Dynamo lug.	M.S.	2
WH.1770	Ignition wire clamp.	Bakelite.	2
WH.1771	Stud.	M.S.	4
	Nut.	M.S.	4
	Spring washers.	Spring S.	4
	Welch washer for ind. pipe.	M.S. 1¼"	2
WH.1773	Balance for induction pipe.	Al.	1
	Oil pipe for rocker feed.	Copper 3/16"O.D. x 1/16" I.D.	
	T-piece for brazing in oil gauge pipe for oil feed to rockers.	Brass to take 3/16" pipe.	1

Standard Swallow 20 hp O.H.V. Conversion Parts List, 1935. Note the name of Weslake in the top left-hand corner.

IKE WEBB, director of Blacknell Sidecars

'I helped to fit the first Swallow sidecar shown at Olympia; year about 1924.

'At that time I was Works Foreman at Brough Superior, and Billy Lyons (as he was then known) was fitting a Swallow sidecar to one of our SS80 models. I had fixed the fittings at the works, but owing to a last minute change at the Show, it was necessary to remove the front taper fitting. Looking on was Mr F.P. Dickson, himself a Brough Superior owner, and well known at the works.

'Mr Lyons was in his shirt sleeves, struggling to unscrew the nut without much success, when Mr Dickson remarked, "I'll bet that's one Ike tightened up! I had better see if he will give you a hand" – which I did, much to Mr Lyon's satisfaction.'

IKE WEBB

This is a curious one. It is clearly a one-off special-bodied S.S.I. Unfortunately the torn-out magazine page, on which I discovered it, has no date or title. Did it come before the SS90 and, if so, did it provide the inspiration?

It is said that Lyons never liked the Airline model, but it sold very well.

Lyons always wanted his cars to be ultra-low and have the longest possible bonnets. It seems that he must have personally instructed the artist who prepared this advertisement!

THE AUTOCAR.   OCTOBER 16TH, 1936.

S. S. JAGUAR

The proved success...
plus 22 new features

S.S. and Jaguar advertising was always bold, colourful, imaginative and beautifully presented. It was one area in which Lyons could be persuaded to spend some money!

THE AUTOCAR.

S. S. J A

As outstanding on the open roa

Already the 1937 S.S. Jaguar has created a profound impression. The inclusion of 22 important features has added both to its acceptedly outstanding performance and to its exclusive refinement. No other car within hundreds of pounds of its price can offer such fascinating ease of handling . . . such safe cornering and roadholding . . . such complete restfulness combined with such responsive vivacity. And surely no car at *any* price can match its coveted individuality of design or — what is perhaps the most important — its unparalleled value.

S.S. CARS LTD., HOLBROOK LANE, COVENTRY (TELEPHONE: COVENTRY 8681)

October 16th, 1936.

The suggestion here seems to be that the name Jaguar only applied to one model, whereas in reality it would henceforth be applied to the whole range.

2½ LITRE SALOON (TAX £15) £385

as it is in the show

New features include wider floor area, increasing leg, foot and seating room. Latest S.U. Automatic carburettors, Tecalemit Oil Filter, New Dunlopillo upholstery. No-draught, winding type half windows in front doors. P.100 lamps. 14″ brakes with new, improved linkage, specially designed brake drums, and Ferodo Racing Type Linings. New engine fittings, greatly increasing silence and smoothness, etc., etc. Arrange for a trial run—when you visit Stand 116, Olympia, or with your local Agent. Literature on request.

LONDON SHOWROOMS: HENLYS, DEVONSHIRE HOUSE, PICCADILLY, W.1 (GROSVENOR 2287)

An SS Jaguar is seen passing through Newton Abbot on the way to Torquay during the 1936 London Rally.

Don't look now, madam, but there is a camera trying to overtake you! (Mrs. E. Simms)

An unusual high-level, period shot of that most rakish of sports cars, the Jaguar SS100.

Cigar smoking comedian, Fred Duprez, takes a close look at the latest product at the 1937 Earls Court Motor Show.

'*The Silent Fast Car*' *sounds suspiciously close to '*The Silent Sports Car*' used by a certain other company.*

'*Lyons dumped about 40 unsold 1935 S.S.Is on the New York agents in February 1936, as "the latest British SS sports cars". It probably paid Lyons to rework the grilles to 1936 standard in case anybody asked awkward questions.*'

ANON

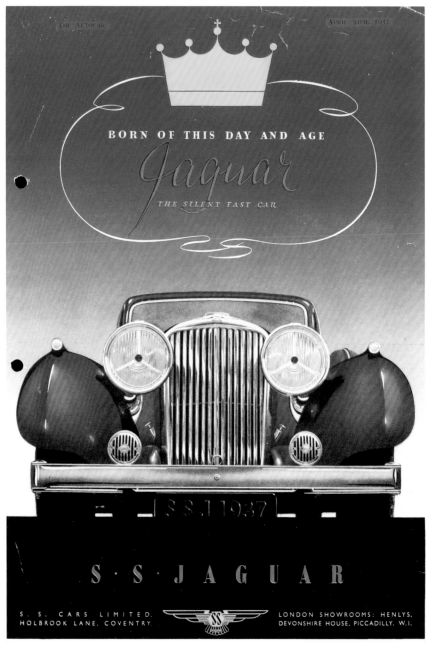

William Walmsley, the man who inspired the Swallow sidecar upon which Jaguar's fortunes were eventually to be built.

Here we see a 1938 1¹/₂-litre chassis photographed at the factory.

THE STANDARD MOTOR CO. LTD.
COVENTRY

TELEGRAMS
FLYWHEEL COVENTRY

TELEPHONE NUMBERS
HEAD OFFICE WORKS
SALES REPAIRS & } NO. 3181
SPARES DEPARTMENTS } (10 LINES)

REGISTERED OFFICE CANLEY, COVENTRY

ALL CODES USED

LONDON SERVICE DEPOT
STANDARD ROAD CHASE ESTATE
PARK ROYAL   N. W. 10.
TELEPHONE No. WILLESDEN 6511

LHD/EC   13th April 1938

Messrs S.S.Cars Ltd
Boleshill
COVENTRY.

ATTENTION: MR.HEYNES

Dear Mr.Heynes,

            Herewith copy of results
of the test of your two Front Springs.

            I felt that you would like
to have all the figures before you when
proceeding with your analysis of the
stiffness of the complete suspension.

                    Yours faithfully,
            For the STANDARD MOTOR CO LTD.,

                    E.Grinham
                    DIRECTOR & CHIEF ENGINEER.

ENCLOSURE

SPRING TEST SHEET   TEST Nº ____

MODEL W.M.H. S.S.1   DRG Nº FRONT SPRINGS   DATE 8 APRIL 38

DISTANCE TESTED (A-B)___ 2"___
            SPRING A   SPRING B

• DOWN_ A 4 - 2 - 12   4 = 3 · 9
        B 9 - 0 - 2   9 - 1 - 18
  DIFF _ 4 - 1 - 18   4 - 2 - 9

UP __ B_ 7 - 3 - 9   7 - 3 - 12
      A 4 - 0 - 2   3 - 3 · 14
  DIFF _ 3 - 3 - 7   3 - 3 - 26

      4 | 8 · 0 · 25   8 · 2 · 7
          2 · 0 · 6   2 · 0 · 15¾

RATE 230 LB/IN   239¾ LB/IN

LADEN LOAD 830 LBS 7 · 1 · 18
            SPRING A   SPRING B.

CAMBER DOWN 15·35   15·16
          UP 15·9"   15·79
AVERAGE CAMBER 15·625"   15·475

CAMBER 3/16" NEG   ⅛" NEG

Grinham and Dawtrey had been young William Heynes's bosses at Humber before they moved to Standard. Subsequently it was they who suggested Heynes to Lyons when the latter was looking to appoint a Chief Engineer for his growing company. With Standard supplying chassis to S.S. Cars, it was natural that they should work together. Note the reference to the new model as the W.M.H. S.S.I.

12 THE AUTOCAR   ADVERTISEMENTS.   JANUARY 29TH, 1937.

JAGUAR

"A name cut deep in the history of modern motoring"

Quality built from end to end, the specification of this fine car challenges comparison with cars costing many times its price. Powerful O.H.V. 6-cylinder Engines; Girling Brakes; Twin Carburettors with automatic starting control; Dunlopillo upholstery; P.100 Headlamps; Adjustable steering wheel; Oversize shock absorbers; Lead coated springs... these are but a few of the features which, allied to superlative performance, make the SS Jaguar the most outstanding car of this generation.

Models and Prices — SS Jaguar 2½ Litre Saloon £385. Tourer £375. "100" Competition Model £395. 1½ Litre Saloon £298.

S.S. CARS LTD., HOLBROOK LANE, COVENTRY. London Showrooms : Henlys, Devonshire House, Piccadilly, W.1.

This must be one of the earliest appearances of the leaping feline, though this one looks more as though he is crawling up an incline!

The Standard Motor Co. supplied the 1776 cc engine after the war to a pre-war order and, in fact, 100 of these were supplied in 1939 for the 1940 season. A further order was received for 6000 of these engines in the forties and these lasted until 1948.

STANDARD-TRIUMPH

Dear old Michael Sedgwick, the late-lamented motoring historian, once referred to the pre-war S.S. Car Club as 'Cads Incorporated'!

COL RIXON BUCKNALL

Builder of the famous 'Red Car', commenting on the Swallow Wolseley Hornet Special of which he had three examples in three years.

'It was a splendid sports car in miniature and was therefore stifled to appease MGs.'

Bill Heynes' personal table of comparative performance figures prepared, presumably, in the late-thirties. (Bill Heynes)

Arthur Whittaker, like Alice Fenton, was a loyal and long serving employee who joined Swallow in the very early days and retired with the position of Vice-Chairman. To him must go much of the credit for Jaguar's ability to offer such remarkable value for money, as there was no more shrewd buyer in the business. (Jaguar Cars)

The bulbous Miles MS7 Aerovan 4 in the background might have benefited from some Lyons styling! The factory SS 100, affectionately known as Old Number 8, was gradually developed to a greater and greater degree, shedding its wings in the process.

Comparative Performance Figures

Make of Car	Bore × Stroke	Capacity	Torque	Weight	Back Axle Ratio	Tyre Size	Spheric Radius	Rev/ft travel	Engine	Flywheel Revs	Road Speed MPH	Tractive Effort	T.E.	
2½L Jag	6 cyl. 73×106	2667	1460	34	4.5	5.50×18	14.35	702	4600	87	457	269		
3½L Jag	6 cyl. 82×114	3485	1920	34	4.25	5.50×18	14.35	702	4600	92	569	**334**		
1½L Jag	4 cyl. 73×106	1775	970	28	4.78	5.25×18	14.15	712	4600	81	327	234		
BMW	''	1775	970	24	4.5	5.25×17	13.5	747	4600	82	324	270		
Vauxhall 14P Six	6 cyl. 61.5×100	1781	972	24¾	4.71	5.50×16	13.00	775	—	71*	353	274		
Vauxhall 12P	4 cyl. 69.5×95	1442	792	21½	4.71	5.25×16	12.70	794	—	65*	294	273		
Bentley 4½L	6 cyl. 89×114	4257	2340	37¾	4.30 overdrive 3.64	6.50×17	14.45	698 —	4450 4050	89* 92*	697 590	369 321		
2½ P.W.			1460	24		6.00×15	13.00	775	4600		316	380		
1½ P.W.			970	23½		6.00×15	13.00	775	4600					
Railton	8 cyl. 76×114	4168	2290	29½	4.1	6.50×16								

An unknown S.S. owner on service S.S.-style.

'When I had my S.S. cars, the works were at Foleshill, Coventry, and I usually collected my cars after repairs on a Sunday.

'On one occasion, the Service Department chief found, just as I was leaving, that my dynamo was not charging. He himself took a dynamo off another car and, as this took time, he invited me to tea at his home, then came along to show me the way out of Coventry, and adjusted the brakes at the roadside, when I stopped and told him they were working unevenly.'

FORTIES

Technical details of the VA and VB wartime prototype lightweight vehicles.

4x2WD ULTRA-LIGHTWEIGHT VEHICLE, MODEL VA

The VA was a three-seater light car with seating for two in the front and one in the back. It was powered by a JAP air-cooled vee-twin engine mounted at the offside rear. The capacity was 1096 cc and, with a 4.7:1 compression ratio, the horsepower was rated at 10.9 and maximum torque was 500 lb/in at 3000 rpm.

The gearbox was mounted above the rear axle, under the engine, and driven by chain, as was the drive from the gearbox to the bevel type differential which was mounted to the body. The diff could be locked by means of a set screw which was put through the final sprocket in the diff unit.

The live swing axle was exposed and had bearing carriers at either end. Lateral location of the rear wheels was provided by the drive axles, side thrust being transmitted back to the bearings in the diff housing.

The rear suspension was independent with coil springs, swing axles, and radius arms providing location and eliminating tramp. The front suspension was also independent by coil springs and steel axle brackets being designed to slide vertically on steering swivel pins. Front and rear track was 4 ft 5 in and the wheelbase was just 2 in longer. The height worked out at 3 ft 6 in and the width at 4 ft 10^1/2 in.

Weights:	Unladen			Laden		
	Cwt	Qtr	lb	Cwt	Qtr	lb
Gross Vehicle Weight	7	3	12	14	1	7
Front Axle Weight	2	2	3	4	0	14
Rear Axle Weight	5	1	9	10	0	21

Pay Load: 3 men plus 250 lb

The vehicle was extremely light and the front end could easily be lifted by one man. The traction was good, owing to most of the weight being concentrated over the driving axle. The VA failed to be reliable, however, due to difficulties with the cooling of the engine and the problem of maintaining the chain drive centres.

A wooden mock-up model and an actual prototype were built, but eventually they were scrapped and work commenced on the second vehicle, the VB which was more conventional in layout.

4x2WD ULTRA-LIGHTWEIGHT VEHICLE, MODEL VB

The VB was a four-seater light car with two seats in the front and two in the rear in the usual manner. It was powered by a Ford 10 water-cooled, side-valve engine mounted in the front. This engine had a capacity of 1172 cc, was, as the name implied a 10 horsepower unit, and produced 30.1 bhp at 4000 rpm on a compression ratio of 6.2:1.

The Ford engine drove through a three-speed, constant mesh gearbox from the same source and had the following ratios: 1st 3.071, 2nd 1.765, 3rd 1.000, reverse 4.015. There was an auxiliary gearbox consisting of an overall reduction gear attached to the output end of the main gearbox. The ratios were 1:1 and 2.083:1. A very short prop shaft took the drive to the bevel drive differential, which was not lockable like that of the VA. Otherwise the rear axle and suspension were similar to the earlier version. The rear axle ratio was 5.375:1.

The front suspension was independent but employed wishbones and coil springs. Tyres of 5.00 in to 5.75 in x 16 were used, those on the rear being of Cross Country tread pattern. The front and rear track was just 4 ft, while wheelbase was 5 ft 1 1/4 in. Overall length amounted to 8 ft and width to 4 ft 6 in. Including the top, height was 6 ft and the VB weighed in at 8 1/2 cwt.

The highly significant feature was, of course, the construction which was unitary. A separate chassis was dispensed with and all stresses were taken by the body construction.

An internal memo from John Silver to Messrs Lyons, Whittaker, Orr and Heynes, dated 13 December 1943 had attached a suggested procedure in connection with post-war development work and makes mention of discussing this at the next Post-War Meeting.

The VA was the first of two small vehicles built by S.S. during the war for dropping by parachute.

SS CARS LIMITED

COVENTRY
ENG.

TELEPHONES
HEAD OFFICE & WORKS
COVENTRY 88681 (10 LINES)
TELEGRAMS: "JAGUAR" COVENTRY
CODE - BENTLEY'S SECOND

DIRECTORS:
W. LYONS,
CHAIRMAN & MANAGING DIRECTOR
T. W. DAFFERN, O.B.E., F.C.A., F.S.A.A.
H. N. GILLITT
A. WHITTAKER, GENERAL MANAGER

YOUR REFERENCE:

OUR REFERENCE:

11th September, 1946

TO MR. LYONS

FROM:- MR. HEYNES

1947-8 PROGRAMME

I am putting forward a few notes on the positions of the 1947-8 programme as previously discussed with you, as a basis for further discussion. I propose we should work along these lines giving this work priority to the exclusion of other experimental work except where this can be worked in without affecting the programme outlined below.
CHASSIS
1. CHASSIS FRAME. The new straight sided box section chassis frame on the lines already existing on the XJ. car will be worked upon. This is considered to be absolutely essential owing to the very poor quality of the frames which we are receiving from Sankey's at the present time. The very wide variation we are getting on the present frames is responsible for a very large number of faults which exist on the present car, and it is anticipated that by a simpler design of frame from the production angle the majority of these will be eliminated even if we have to put up with the same source of manufacture.
2. FRONT SUSPENSION. Independent suspension basically as at present fitted to the XJ. chassis. Experiments are now in hand with softer rubber bushes to reduce the hysteresis or internal friction in the system, which will give the effect of a softer ride without having to reduce any further the rate of the springs, which theoretically are as low as those used on the majority of American cars, but which give the false rating by this internal stiffness.

Designs are now in hand which replace the top wishbone by the Armstrong or Luvax shock absorber which eliminates the further working part.

Stub axle, wheel bearings, hub, ball pivots, and steering linkage all appear to be perfectly satisfactory, and will remain unchanged.

Experiments are being tried out with a slightly increased offset on the wheel by means of packing pieces, as we feel that due to the wide section of the tyre we are rather too close to the centre point steering position than is desirable.

Adjustment of bottom wishbone bushes to the frame and also the mounting for the shock absorber are being incorporated to the single bracket, which will be an integral part of the frame dispensing with the use of the bolt-on brackets now employed.

3. STEERING. The worm and rack steering at present employed will be retained basically subject to modifications to eliminate faults which exist in its present state.

(a) HEAVINESS. The pinion which started off with 10 teeth and has now been reduced to 8 is now being reduced to 7 teeth, which gives us the affect of a further $12^1/2$% lighter steering than we have at present, which we feel should be satisfactory. In addition to this, with the new steering box design the pinion is mounted on roller bearings which may give anything up to another 20% lightness.

(b) The slight coarseness which can be felt is considered to be due to the straight tooth rack and pinion, and the helical gear and rack are being used to enable us to obtain a greater tooth overlap which will eliminate this point.

(c) STEERING WHEEL KICK. By the modifications which have already been carried out this has been reduced to a very large extent, and may possibly be eliminated entirely by the increased offset which we are giving the front wheels experimentally. On the other hand a steering box of a revised design is being constructed under Burman Patents with a variable reverse efficiency which should entirely eliminate any reaction being felt on the steering wheel, and yet retain exceptional lightness on the actual steering control.

4. REAR SUSPENSION. The rear suspension which is being tried out on the XJ. at the moment shows considerable promise for axle location, and appears to be generally satisfactory except we have not so far succeeded in eliminating the friction in the system to give us the soft ride which we require. Experiments are being carried out mounting the main arm on roller and ball bearings in an endeavour to obtain a floating ride, but it is not considered desirable with this bearing set up for production, and it is felt that considerable further experimental work and a certain amount of re-design is necessary before the system is perfected to a state where we can release it for production.

An alternative design in body and semi-elliptic leaf springs carried on the frame extension has been prepared, and it is proposed to proceed with this as a basis of the production model.

The axle is being mounted on to the leaf spring through rubber bushes and will be controlled for torque reaction by means of the shock absorber arms situated well above the axle centre. By this means we can retain the low prop shaft tunnel which was obtained with the torsion bar suspension, and we have a system which follows closely on the conventional practice and eliminates the necessity for extensive experimental work.

5. SHOCK ABSORBERS. Front shock absorbers as already stated under front suspension will be made an integral part of the top wishbone. The Armstrong shock absorber is the most convenient type for our purpose, and a design is being made primarily to suit this shock absorber.

REAR SHOCK ABSORBER. Here again the arm of the shock absorber will also form a torque control arm for the rear axle.

An S.S. Cars internal report, prepared in September 1944, and entitled 'Development and Design on Current Models not applicable to 1st Release', makes mention of the introduction of a $1^1/2$ litre SS100.

MANAGING DIRECTOR'S OFFICE

TELEPHONE 88681 (10 LINES)
TELEGRAMS 'JAGUAR' COVENTRY

SS
WORKS
HOLBROOK LANE
COVENTRY

30th December, 1944

It is the Company's desire to establish a means of added remuneration to members of the Staff whose initiative, loyalty and efficiency mean so much to the prosperity of the Company, and a new scheme providing additional payments to existing salary is to be put into operation immediately.

These payments will be dependent upon and directly related to the Company's annual profits in accordance with a schedule setting out the percentage payable in relation to profits, which is now in course of preparation, and will be issued immediately on completion.

Although the profits of the Company are not yet available, the incidence of E.P.T. makes it possible to provide an estimate sufficiently accurate to indicate the appropriate percentage.

As a member of the Staff eligible to participate in this scheme, you will receive immediately the first provisional payment of a sum represented by 20% of your existing salary, and this will continue to be paid to you until you receive notification of adjustment.

Members of the Staff who may leave the Company's employ or become redundant shall not be entitled to any payment under this scheme exceeding that due for a period of one month.

W. Lyons.

A letter from Lyons advising staff that a bonus was to be paid.

A customer visiting the works on one occasion saw Lyons and said to him, 'You know I wish you'd discard your rubber top to the gear lever – it gets hot and sticky, and makes your hand black'.

Lyons, who did not take kindly to complaints, put the fellow in his place by replying with the stinging retort, 'Gentlemen usually drive in gloves'!

Armstrong type shock absorbers will be used on the first set-up, but provision can easily be made here for either type.

6. (a) LOCKHEED BRAKES. Due to the use of 16″ tyres we are tied to using a maximum drum diameter on the brakes of 12″. The first set of brakes fitted up on this car are Lockheed 12″ x 1⅝″ and are fitted with VG.91 linings. The brakes can be faded under exacting conditions. This is believed not to be actual lining fade, but rather due to drum expansion and the high leverage giving insufficient travel at the brake shoe to take care of this. The pedal reaches the floor board after three fairly high speed applications, but apparently the effectiveness quickly returns.

The feel of the brakes, however, is entirely unsatisfactory. They lack the 'bite' which we have on the present production 14″ brakes. These brakes have been demonstrated to Messrs. Lockheed and we are awaiting their further remarks.

It may be possible that the trouble can be overcome by fitting an automatic adjuster which will allow us to run a reduced amount of free travel on the pedal, but Lockheed are not in a position to supply this at the moment, consequently our experiments on Lockheed brakes are in abeyance.

(b) GIRLING BRAKES. We have just received the first experimental set of Girling brakes for this car. These are the 12″ x 1⅝″. The question of fitting a wider brake is at present being looked into in the Drawing Office, as it is felt that this will probably be necessary for the 2½ and 3½-litre car.

These brakes are the hydrostatic type 2 L.S. on the front and normal type on the rear. Owing to the self-adjusting properties of the hydrostatic brake a higher pedal ratio will be possible than has been permissible with the Lockheed brakes which we have been trying, and it is thought that satisfactory results can be obtained without further modification. A report on these brakes should be available in about a fortnight's time.

Making general reference to the self-adjustment, I have made it perfectly clear to both Girling and Lockheed that under no circumstances will we consider the manually adjusted brake for our new designs. I feel that this attitude is quite justified in view of the fact that the Americans will have had at least 2 years experience on self-adjusting brakes.

7. WHEELS. Wheels so far supplied by Dunlops have been unsatisfactory. Difficulty is experienced on removing and refitting the tyres, partly due to the shallow-based rim, and partly due to the tyre construction. It is confidently expected, however, that we shall be clear of this difficulty by the time production is ready to commence.

On the experimental wheels submitted, breakage has been experienced in the disc pressing. These have cracked at the bottom of the main bowl due to the wheel flexing under load. Dunlops are investigating this and we are expecting further sample wheels at an early date.

The tyre size 6.00 x 16" appears to be adequate for our requirements on the Saloon, and it is proposed to retain this size.

8. PROPELLER SHAFT. The divided Prop. Shaft is essential to obtain the low floor line which we require. So far our experience with this has been unsatisfactory. We have not been able to entirely eliminate Prop. Shaft vibration. Experiments are still proceeding on the lines of known practise. Drawings have been obtained of the centre joint used on the 25 h.p. Wolseley, and the question has been discussed with Mr. Van Eugan of Wolseley's. Apparently their experience was that the rubber requires to be very hard and very little of it to give the best results. This is contrary to what one would expect, but we have had the same indication from Messrs. Hardy Spicer, possibly derived from their joint experiments at Wolseley's. Experiments are proceeding, and it is anticipated that the question will be cleared by trial and error.

9. BODY MOUNTING. On the second XJ. chassis on which the design is proceeding, arrangements will be made in conjunction with Body Design to mount the body alongside the outside of the front members on rubber pads as we saw employed on the 1946 Chrysler. The question of this mounting is only just being picked up, and it is too early to give details as to how this will be carried out.

ENGINE

1.6 CYLINDER ENGINE (3$\frac{1}{2}$ and 2$\frac{1}{2}$-LITRE). It is proposed that for the commencement of production the present 6 cylinder engine should be employed. Provision is naturally being made on the car to accommodate the new engine as an alternative, but it is felt that if experiments on the new engine do not prove immediately successful when the first engine is completed, the position might be set back so that production of the 6 cylinder engine cannot be achieved in time to meet the production requirements.

2$\frac{1}{2}$-LITRE ENGINE. With the supply of the present 1$\frac{1}{2}$-litre engine ceasing, it is essential that an alternative engine is available at the time production starts. Two alternatives are being considered here. Either the 4 cylinder XK engine to be brought into production from the start, or an alternative small 6 cylinder (1900 c.c.) engine on the present 2$\frac{1}{2}$-litre block can be made available subject to satisfactory engines of this type being produced experimentally.

(a) 1900 c.c. 6 CYLINDER ENGINE. Preliminary tests on this engine have indicated that the engine has possibilities, but the re-design of head and induction passages would be necessary to obtain the desired H.P., particularly at the bottom end. A cylinder head design is being *prepared which I consider would be desirable to produce in aluminium, and it would be modified in such a way that it would allow the use of the flat top piston. The cylinder block would be maintained identical with the 2¹/₂ litre cylinder block.*

If this is done, it is suggested that the machining of this cylinder head should be put out to avoid further loading up of the tooling position on our own shops.

(b) XK 4 CYLINDER ENGINE. Bench experiments on this engine are still proceeding, and although the engine shows considerable improvement over our present range of engines, it is still not up to the standard which we consider desirable before this is released. It is, however, felt that in the main the results can be produced without major modification. The bottom half of the engine so far has stood up considerably better than any other engine which we have had.

No major trouble has been experienced with the aluminium head, the valve seats, the valve gear generally, or with their ability to withstand the prolonged running.

The chain drives at the front of the engine have not yet been tested in their latest form, but experience with the XF engine and the greater simplicity of the drive which has now been achieved indicates that we are justified in expecting a silent, satisfactory operation at this point.

The final decision on this must await the first engine of the present second series engines.

The combustion chamber design appears to be the one thing which is not really as yet 100% satisfactory. The engine with the latest combustion head has been submitted to Mr. Weslake who is about to commence a further series of tests.

Our own feeling on this combustion chamber is that the compression pressures which are being obtained with the 7¹/₂:1 compression ratio are satisfactory. The power output, however, from these compression pressures is disappointing, and the tendency to detonation which we are experiencing is unsatisfactory in view of the fact that we are using an aluminium head with an excellent water flow and 80 octane fuel. It is our opinion that the engine should operate satisfactorily under these conditions without pinking, with at least 8:1 compression ratio, and that it is due to unsatisfactory burning in some way which is preventing us from getting the desired results.

We are at the moment experimenting with the method of reducing the inlet gas blow over the head of the hot exhaust valve. We have in addition placed on order a set of salt cooled valves, and if either of these experiments show an effective increase of B.M.E.P., I anticipate that we shall be able to remedy the trouble very quickly and with very little alteration.

Alternatively, or pending the correction of the burning in this head, it would be quite satisfactory to go into production with this engine with a 7:1 compression ratio, and the engine would still give a very much superior performance than that which is produced by our present 1¹/₂ litre engine. In addition, there is considerable saving in weight on this engine as compared with our present unit.

GEARBOX

The position on the gearbox still remains rather open and the following alternatives are listed for further discussion together with comments on their respective merits.

(a) EXISTING SYNCHROMESH GEARBOX WITH SINGLE HELICAL GEARS. The latest sample box manufactured by Moss does indicate that this can be made satisfactorily and it may be advisable to continue fitting this box on the six cylinder cars to maintain production, or at any rate it can be viewed as an alternative. It is considered that this box is unnecessarily heavy for the 1¹/₂-litre.

(b) INERTIA LOCK SYNCHROMESH. If the re-design of the synchromesh was made to improve synchronising and the box made

suitable for all sizes of engine, we would propose to go to inertia lock type of synchromesh, either using the modification of the Buick such as we used on the Hillman Minx, which is quite satisfactory, or manufacturing the later General Motors type under licence. This would involve a royalty of somewhere between 8/- [40p] and 12/- [60p] per box, which I consider excessive and I would suggest that if the box is re-designed, an inertia lock unit of both types is made up so that we may see exactly what we are getting for the royalty payment.

(c) COTAL GEARBOX. Discussions with Mr. Van Eugan at Wolseley's indicate that quite a lot of development work has taken place on this box, which has resulted in reduction in weight and a slight reduction in size.

This '100' driver and his riding companion seem to be in a state of some consternation and concern with regard to the rear of the motor car. Or, perhaps he has just run somebody over!

The sizes of boxes which they are making 10/12 m.k.g. (84 ft. lbs.) and 18 m.k.g. (35 ft. lbs.) would be suitable for the $1\frac{1}{2}$-litre and the $2\frac{1}{2}$-litre respectively. For the $3\frac{1}{2}$-litre engine, however, we should fit a 25 m.k.g. box which they do not propose to manufacture, and to obtain a box of this capacity we should either have to go direct to France and buy boxes complete, which is liable to be extremely difficult, or endeavour to obtain a licence to manufacture for ourselves or someone else to manufacture for us.

The most difficult problem here appears to be the fact that whilst we can obtain boxes for the smaller engines, for the larger car we should be faced with using either a normal synchromesh box or an 18 m.k.g. box, which would really be rather over-stressed, but which might prove satisfactory in practice. It is possible that an improvement in the quality of the gear steel could be made which would enable us to successfully use an 18 m.k.g. box with a 3^1/$_2$-litre engine. This would need investigation which should really be carried out by a parent company.

(d) DE NORMANVILLE BOX. The 4 speed De Normanville box has distinct possibilities providing it can be manufactured economically and that it proves sufficiently reliable in operation. I see no reason why both these requirements should not be made providing sufficient energy is put behind the development of the box from this stage.

The first 2 speed box will be available for trial in the course of a few days, and if we are satisfied with this we should propose asking De Normanville to push right ahead with the 4 speed box. If this box were adopted, I think it should be introduced at first as an optional extra to the normal synchromesh box until we had 12 months experience of it in the hands of the public.

CLUTCH

A number of experiments are in hand on the clutch to try and improve the pick up, particularly after a reasonable mileage and also to prevent interference due to engine movement and transmission noise to the car, and in addition to obtain a considerably lighter pedal than that which we have at the moment.

Designs are being prepared in conjunction with Messrs. Lockheed for an hydraulic operation. Progress, however, on this is very slow. In the meantime, an alternative pedal operation has been developed and is being fitted on our left hand drive cars, which from initial tests on the 1^1/$_2$-litre appears to be quite effective and it may be more satisfactory to adopt this method of operation than to go to the hydraulic type.

On the clutch plate we are pressing as hard as possible to obtain a rubber centre to try out the value of this on the reduction of transmission noises.

A Borglite plate and various types of lining material are also being experimented with. The results, however, so far have been rather mixed.

REAR AXLE (HARDY SPICER MANUFACTURE)

The position regarding the supply of the Spicer axle is still not quite clear. I understand it will be a considerable time before they are able to manufacture in this country, and it does seem essential that an alternative source of supply is obtained. Probably the best plan would be to have one firm alternative for the small axle and another firm for the large unit. Moss and E.N.V. Engineering are the two firms under consideration at the moment.

In view of the present delay in getting the major tools produced and new designs into operation, it appears that we shall be faced with the necessity of carrying on with the existing 1945 body for at least 12 months following the 1947 Show, unless we consider manufacturing a new body built up as at present from small panels or changing back to the coach-built body. Circumstances may prove it desirable to produce a coach-built body for the 3^1/$_2$-litre only to the new design continuing on the main production lines with the present steel body with certain modifications. The following suggestions are put forward assuming that we are continuing with this body for a further 12 months.

1. BODY MOUNTING. To obtain a greater silence in the car it appears desirable to go to a rubber mounting between the frame and the bottom sill of the body such as was used on the 1946 Chrysler. To do this the bottom side of the body would require modifying and considerably stiffening. The single piece rocker from front to rear is most desirable and general strengthening up particularly around the centre pillar can also be carried out at the same time. In addition to this the floors would have to be self-supporting off the bottom side as contact with the chassis frame except through rubber would be avoided.

2. FLOATING DASH. The present floating dash lacks the stiffness which we had on the 1937 type dash. The accessibility to the instrument panel and the mounting of the battery are unsatisfactory. With

Sir William Lyons was visiting the Piccadilly showrooms one day when he was approached by the Sales Manager.

'Excuse me, Sir William. The carpets in the showroom are becoming very worn, and threadbare in places. May I order new carpets?'

'Certainly not,' replied Lyons, who was not known for spending money unnecessarily. 'There is plenty of wear left in those.'

That was the end of the conversation. On a subsequent visit a month or two later, however, Lyons happened to look down and noticed – new carpet! The unfortunate fellow was summoned.

'I thought I told you not to replace the carpet. I thought I told you that the existing ones were perfectly satisfactory. When I give an order, I expect it to be obeyed . . .'

Lyons carried on in this vein until the fellow managed to interrupt long enough to explain that they weren't new carpets.

'What I have done, Sir William, is to turn them round. Half of each strip was under the show cabinets at the side of the room, and therefore not worn. So now that I have reversed them the worn area is under the cabinets.'

Lyons was silent for a few moments, as he looked around him. The young man held his breath.

'Remarkable,' muttered Lyons. 'Remarkable.'

There was another pause.

'Right, my man. I want you at Wappenbury Hall, nine o'clock on Monday morning. You can do the same thing for me at home.'

---

modification to these items an improvement in the pedals and general sealing would be affected at the same time, and an endeavour to obtain a little more footroom for the pedals would also be made. Mounting for the heater and wireless would be considerably simplified, so that these units could be replaced from under the bonnet rather than the inside of the car.

3. WEIGHT SAVING. Whilst the main structure of the body would be kept in steel, experiments on the use of aluminium should be carried out immediately on such components as front and rear doors, sliding roof, bootlid, number plate lid, and lining boards in the rear boot.

4. BONNET. Fixed bonnet sides without louvres to be experimented with. The valences under the front wing to be across the wing as a diaphragm to support the wing and also to allow a clear flow of air over the engine to the inside of the wing and avoid a pressure build up on it.

5. INSTRUMENTS AND ACCESSORIES. Instrument panel to be restyled raising it to allow more clearance for the driver's knees, and if possible further forward to give a more spacious appearance in the front seats.

SCREEN WIPERS. Cable operated type to be considered in conjunction with self-parking as on American cars. We suggest here that we should consider the fitting of a fixed screen both to facilitate production and to eliminate difficulties of screen wiper parking.

Collision looks imminent for this SS 100 driver!

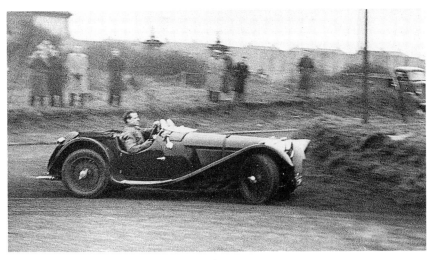

Heater and air conditioning unit needs an entire re-design. Views on this have already been expressed to Clayton Dewandre.

Instruments can be made either easily detachable from the rear or detachable by lifting the facia panel in which case all wiring to be on the front of the instrument wiring panel so that it is immediately accessible.

6. SEATS. The front seats need a complete re-design, firstly to reduce the weight, and secondly to incorporate an effective sliding and lifting mechanism which can be easily operated.

Was this photograph, which I discovered in Bill Heynes' files, the inspiration for the 'rotund style' Jaguar? It was a projected V8 Claveau. Emile Claveau, a Frenchman, who is described in Nick Georgano's definitive encyclopedia as, 'an experimenter rather than a manufacturer,' was building monocoque designs with all-independent suspension as early as 1926, and built this creation in 1946.

FROM MANAGING DIRECTOR
21st September, 1946

To MR. HEYNES
Herewith my notes on your report dated the 11th September.

1947 – 8 PROGRAMME

CHASSIS
1. Before a decision can be made to adopt the new frame for the existing body, purchase commitments must be carefully investigated of all material affected.
2. FRONT SUSPENSION. The precaution necessary in the case of the Frame is necessary also here. I feel that the progress that has been made with this suspension is most disappointing. I do not think there is a sufficiently concentrated effort. I cannot see that we have any chance at the present rate of progress, of introducing this chassis next year.
I would, however, like a definite timetable of the further development work intended.
3. STEERING. As number 2. Unless we can achieve a steering to compare with the PACKARD at an early date we must proceed with a steering identical to the PACKARD.
4. REAR SUSPENSION. I am in agreement with this, but feel it is possibly a retrograde step. Here again I would like a timetable.
5. SHOCK ABSORBERS. This I agree.
6. LOCKHEED BRAKES. Agreed.
7. WHEELS. The question of road drum must be considered.
8. PROPELLER SHAFT. Agreed.
9. BODY MOUNTING. Agreed.

ENGINE
1. 6 CYLINDER ENGINE (3^{1}/$_{2}$ and 2^{1}/$_{2}$-LITRE). Agreed.
2. 1^{1}/$_{2}$-litre ENGINE. Agreed: but the question of 4 cylinder to be produced off the existing tooling and plant must also be investigated. The XK must undoubtedly be 100% before it is passed to production, the first XF operated satisfactorily at 8:1 compression, so we should not forego the advantage we gained.

GEARBOX
*a) EXISTING SYNCHRONISER GEARBOX WITH SINGLE
HELICAL GEARS. We should persevere to obtain quietness and easy
gear change with the existing double helical, and at the same time push
forward with the single helical providing we are satisfied they will stand
up.*
*b) INERTIA LOCK SYNCHROMESH. The cost of tooling up, and
length of time is of the greatest importance.*
*c) COTAL GEARBOX. We should proceed with this as far and as
quickly as possible. The question of the ordinary synchromesh for the
small engine must also be taken up as quickly as possible with
Wolseley's.*
*d) DE NORMANVILLE BOX. If we could prove this quickly, the
question of manufacture would have to be investigated.*

CLUTCH
*There is room for considerable improvement and this should be
persevered with.*

REAR AXLE (Hardy Spicer manufacture)
We are obtaining quotations.

BODY
*We must at this juncture assume that we shall continue with the present
body.*
*1. BODY MOUNTING. No change must be made without firstly fully
investigating what they involve, but I agree the principle.*
*2. FLOATING DASH. Agreed. The question of Heat must also be
considered.*
*3. WEIGHT SAVING. Here again the consequences of a change must
be considered.*
4. BONNET. Agreed.
*5. INSTRUMENTS AND ACCESSORIES. Agreed. But the existing
opening screen to be retained.*
6. SEATS. Agreed.

**BOARD MEETING,
14 AUGUST 1947**
The Chairman reported that he had made an offer to acquire the name Lagonda, goodwill, jigs, tools, drawings, patents, all cars, car stocks, spares and service equipment, for the sum of £85,000. Up to the time of this meeting no reply had yet been received.

*G.F.A. Gale in his SS Jaguar 100
takes on and beats Sarginson in his
MG in the over-2-litre class for
standard sports cars at the Brighton
Speed Trials in 1947.*

Caravan manufacturers Sprite Ltd, undertook a 10,000 mile tour with one of their caravans towed by a 1948 3$^{1}/_{2}$-litre Jaguar saloon. Apart from a broken exhaust manifold due to the uneven roads, the trip was trouble-free, but Jaguar declined to use the exploit for their publicity purposes.

One of the directors of the company later wrote to a colleague, of the exercise. No assistance was given by Jaguar, for if you remember, the words of Lofty England at the time were, "The ruddy things should not be allowed on the road".

Well said, Lofty!

April 20th, 1949

To MR. LYONS
Copies to MR. HEYNES, MR. BAILY, AND MR. RANKIN.

XK 2-SEATER

SPEED TESTS ON JABBEKE ROAD, BELGIUM
The car was tested over a mile on a perfectly level stretch of the Jabbeke road, this being the same section used by Col. Gardner for his recent records, and to ensure the accuracy of the measured distance, his timing marks were utilised.

The stopwatch was operated by an observer carried in the car, as electrical timing not being available, any system of flag signalling would have proved too inaccurate over a mile.

A check test of rpm with and without the observer showed that his weight had no effect upon the speed. The faster time recorded on Test 5 was entirely due to the improved streamlining resulting from fitting the tonneau cover.

Clark Gable taking delivery of his new XK120; or perhaps he went everywhere like this! (Jaguar Cars)

BOARD MEETING, 9 OCTOBER 1947

Lagonda: The Chairman reported that our offer to Lagonda had not been accepted.

The figures, with the exceptions of Tests 4 and 5, represent the mean of two or more runs in each direction. Tests 4 and 5 were taken in one direction only, as on the other I was driving directly into the sun, and there being a considerable amount of traffic on the road, it was desirable to have good visibility. The speeds recorded can, however, be taken as a mean, the road being quite level and the following wind only slight.

An observer could not be carried on Test 5, but it was possible to make an accurate assessment of the speed by comparing the rpm with those recorded on the previous run. On the official tests, when electrical timing will be used it will, of course, not be necessary to carry an observer, and, the road being closed, weather conditions will not be of much importance.

Particulars of the tests are as follows:-
Tyres Dunlop R.S. 6.00 x 16. Pressures 35 lbs., front & rear (cold)

TEST	CONDITION	SPEED
I	Standard. Hood down.	120.0 mph
II	Undershield fitted. Hood down.	123.25 mph
III	Undershield fitted. Hood & side curtains erected.	125.0 mph
IV	Undershield fitted. Screen removed, cockpit open (rpm 5700 true)	131.3 mph
V	Undershield fitted. Screen removed, tonneau cover fitted (rpm 5900 true)	135.0 mph

The car held the road very well indeed. Slight instability at speeds in excess of 125 mph was counteracted by carrying a full Jerry can in the boot, this making a considerable improvement. Tests with and without the Jerry can showed that it did not detract from the speed.

At cruising and high speeds the engine maintained a temperature of 70 – 80 degrees C, but in London traffic blocks the temperature rose to boiling point. A run of half a mile, at 30 mph was then sufficient to reduce it to 90 degrees C.

The brake linings (V.G. 91) are some improvement on those previously tried out on the Two-Seater, but they are commencing to judder badly, and it will be necessary to carry out further experiments before the brakes can be considered satisfactory.

If it is decided to fit an undershield as standard some ventilation will be required in order to maintain the sump and gearbox temperatures within safe limits. The driving compartment also becomes very hot. The seats, particularly the cushions, are uncomfortable on a long run.

FIFTIES

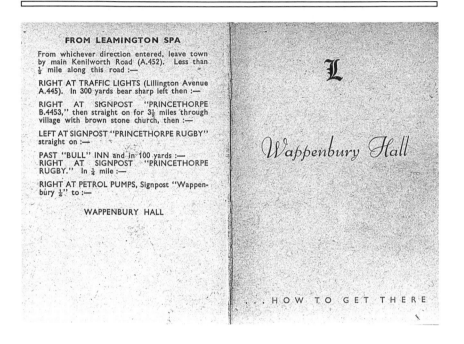

FROM LEAMINGTON SPA

From whichever direction entered, leave town by main Kenilworth Road (A.452). Less than ½ mile along this road :—

RIGHT AT TRAFFIC LIGHTS (Lillington Avenue A.445). In 300 yards bear sharp left then :—

RIGHT AT SIGNPOST "PRINCETHORPE B.4453," then straight on for 3½ miles through village with brown stone church, then :—

LEFT AT SIGNPOST "PRINCETHORPE RUGBY" straight on :—

PAST "BULL" INN and in 100 yards :—
RIGHT AT SIGNPOST "PRINCETHORPE RUGBY." In ¼ mile :—

RIGHT AT PETROL PUMPS, Signpost "Wappenbury ¼" to :—

WAPPENBURY HALL

Wappenbury Hall

... HOW TO GET THERE

According to an internal memo dated 1 September 1950, the new sports racing car to be designed for the 1951 Le Mans was to be known as the XK.150. Instead it became the XK120C, or entirely unofficially, the C-type.

If one remembers that the XK120 was so-called to indicate the car's estimated top speed, then the choice of XK.150 was an entirely logical one.

At this date, it was intended to use a chassis of 'two main basic tubes and basic front cross member and rear cross member. Tubular centre cross member and tubular upper frame side members would be suitable either for the body to conform to the International Sports Car Regulations, or with straight tubes which would permit the construction of a monoposto body'.

This chassis was to be designed to take no less than seven different engines, including the XK.100.

By December the specification had evolved to that which was to be produced and the frame was now described as 'tubular, of triangulated construction'.

On this report the '150' was crossed out and '120C' was written above.

Official speeds recorded over timed kilometre during the Tourist Trophy Race of 1951, as issued by the RAC.

Collins	Allard 5.4-litre	110.30 mph
Allard	Allard 5.4-litre	110.90
Watkins	Allard 4-litre	101.90
Moss	Jaguar XK.120.C	127.60
Walker	Jaguar XK.120.C	128.20
Rolt	Jaguar XK.120.C	127.40
Fairman	Jaguar XK.120	115.60
Swift	Jaguar XK.120	111.50
Macklin	Aston Martin D.B.3	114.90

Abecassis	Aston Martin D.B.2	110.50
Shawe-Taylor	Aston Martin D.B.2	110.50
Clark	Aston Martin D.B.2	107.00
Buncombe	Healey	103.60
Baird	Ferrari 2.6-litre	121.20
Lee	Connaught 1750 c.c.	107.40
Gerard	Frazer Nash 2-litre	109.10

Wappenbury Hall, Lyons's magnificent home and backdrop for many photographs of Jaguar models, 'was originally bought for just £5000'. Rankin let that slip on one occasion,' the late Claude Baily once mentioned to me.

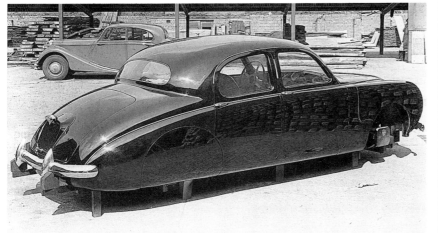

Lyons always referred to the Mark I, which we see here in earliest mock-up form, as the 'rotund style'. It is interesting to note that the wing styling atop the headlamps is reminiscent of the later S-type and even the XJ6. Also it appears that the whole front end was to be a one-piece item hinging forward akin to the E-type. (Jaguar Cars)

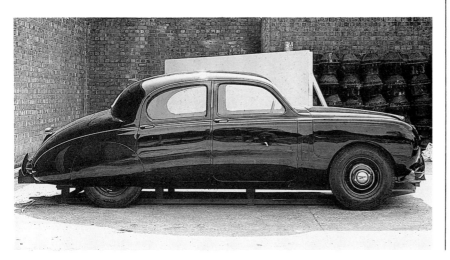

Behind this view of the trim shop can be seen an XK120 Roadster, a Drophead Mark V and several Mark V Saloons. (Jaguar Cars)

One of the main exhibits on the 1952 Earls Court Show stand was the 'Seven Days and Nights' car, LWK 707.

Financial arrangements made with Stirling Moss for the 1951 season

22nd September, 1950

STIRLING MOSS

£100 per drive plus reasonable personal hotel expenses in the case of British and Continental races. In the case of American, or races that necessitated exceptional expenses, special arrangements would have to be made. Prize money and bonus money would be retained by the driver.

Entry to be made by the driver, on the Company's instruction, in any race of the Company's choice. On the other hand Mr. Moss will agree to give us priority of his services as a driver in any race open to sports cars in which we may choose to participate. This would, of course, not preclude Mr. Moss from taking part in formula racing or 500 c.c. racing with other makes of vehicle.

The car to be raced would be loaned to Mr. Moss as his property, but would remain in control of the Company at all times other than when actually participating in events.

'Sir William Lyons was a man of complete integrity in every sense of the word.'

ALAN NEWSOME

Shell celebrates the XK120's remarkable feat of achieving 172 mph at Jabbeke in 1952 in their own inimitable and truly delightful way. (Shell)

Telephone 2181

White Cloud Farm
Tring, Herts

Dear Mr Heynes

I would like to say how excellently the X.K. performed at Silverstone. Its preparation was perfect, and I cannot find one word to say against it at all.

I am sorry about our misfortune in the Mille Miglia, but it could not be avoided; it would have taken a Nuvolari to sort that one out!

I'm enclosing my expense a/c for the M. Miglia etc.

Sincerely yours

Stirling

10th May, 1951

Dear Stirling,

Many thanks for your letter of the 7th enclosing your account.

I was just as sorry as you are about the Mille Miglia, but we have to take the rough with the smooth in matters like this.

I must congratulate you again on the very successful drive at Silverstone, and trust the same good luck will follow you throughout the season.

Yours sincerely,

Shell salutes the XK120's achievements at Montlhéry. (Shell)

Internal memo from CLAUDE BAILY to Messrs Whittaker, Heynes, Blumson, Weaver, Cook and Siviter, 9 January 1952

HUBS FOR KNOCK ON WIRE WHEELS C.6021/1 FRONT. C.6022/3 REAR

XK120 CARS

Mr. Turner can provide 22 sets of Front and Rear hubs ex XK120C finished stock, for the building of twelve XK120 cars and ten XK120C cars. These hubs are made from some stampings which they had in stock (not Jaguar) and in the case of the front hub an additional ring had to be welded on to make up the required length.

The new dies and stampings are said to be still some twelve months away, so that a further covering order is necessary to bring up the total quantity of these hubs to the fifty sets for XK120C cars and including our further anticipated requirements on the XK120 car.

[From this we can see how few of the earlier 120s left the factory with wire wheels in spite of the high proportion wearing them today. *P.P.*]

BOARD MEETING 2 January 1952

BROWNS LANE – Mr. Lyons reported that he had completed negotiations with the Ministry of Supply regarding the rent for the Browns Lane factory. A draft lease was being examined. This provided for taking over the factory from August 1st 1951 – the first five months to December, 1951 to be rent free, and then the lease would be for ten years from January 1st, 1952. Rent to be £30,000 per annum for the first five years, and £57,500 for the last five years.

The following was quoted from a letter from Sir Archibald Rowlands of the Ministry. 'In the event of altering the whole basis of rentals for Government owned factories, then you will get the benefit which may result therefrom. This would be in addition to the special concessions already made to you arising out of the special circumstances of your own case.'

Daily Mail. Monday 25 June 1951. The Jaguar XK120C, the new Le Mans version of the world's fastest-cheapest sports car, is "practically in production and assured of an enormous sale," Mr. Claude Baily, chief designer of Jaguar Cars Ltd. said last night. "Practically every one we turn out will be for export," he added.

Stirling Moss is seen hurling the big Mark VII round the Silverstone circuit in 1952 to win the Production Car Race. (Frank Rainbow)

This was accepted in the event of any other factories being let on more favourable terms which had received comparable treatment, as this answer was in response to the Chairman's specific request.

Although it had been hoped we should be completely installed in Browns Lane by the end of last year, due to slowness of the exit of the Daimler Company, this was not possible but the move should be completed within the next three or four months.

Arrangements are being made to provide a sports field to replace that now sold to Dunlop. We have been successful in obtaining a lease for a piece of land from Coventry Corporation at a rental of £30 per annum, the lease to coincide with the lease of Browns Lane Factory.

Mr, Lyons reported that we had now received official advice that a contract from the Ministry of Supply for the manufacture of Meteor tank engines is to be placed with us. In this connection we have received a contract for the purchase of material to the value of one million pounds. We have also received a contract for the repair of Meteor tank engines. These contracts might prove nearly as large a part of the Company's business as that of car manufacturer.

In connection with the manufacturing contract a lot of the machines have already arrived at the Browns Lane factory from the Ministry of Supply on a rental basis. The ultimate value of plant so provided would be in the region of three million pounds. Rental terms appeared satisfactory but these were receiving consideration.

It was also reported that information had been received that a contract for development of a prototype tank engine, Jaguar XK.800, will be placed with the company by the Ministry of Supply.

Directors' visit to America: Messrs. Whittaker and Heynes had been to the United States of America. They visited most of the car manufacturing plants where they had high level technical discussions obtaining much knowledge of the highest value to the Company.

They also visited our distributors in New York and Los Angeles where they met many Jaguar dealers and discussed both present and future prospects for the sale of the Company's products.

Exports: Mr. Lyons reported that we had had a very successful year in regard to export and read out the monthly figures. These show that the total exports for the year ended December 1st, 1951 were 84.35% of production. Home deliveries have been kept to the figures laid down, with the result that we received a small bonus on sheet supplies.

Report on Jaguar Mark VII KRW 76

15th May, 1952
To Mr. ENGLAND

From R.E. BERRY
GENERAL

Total Distance Covered	*6437 kms*
Total Petrol Consumed	*1076 litres*
Overall Petrol Consumption	*17 mpg*
Total Oil Added to Sump	*8 litres*

The overall petrol consumption figure is interesting since it is the result of widely varying conditions of driving from the 50 mph gait of our outward run to the 90 mph cruising along the autostrada, and the pottering around Brescia.
REPORT

This was the same car in which we covered some 4700 kilometres during the period of the Monte Carlo Rally.

A considerable amount of work appeared to have been done on the car since it was last used by us, this being particularly noticeable in the engine which was extremely quiet, and produced much more power than in January. Carrying all the spares required for the "C" car plus four wheels and tyres, the luggage of four persons, and two passengers, the car was very heavily laden and must have weighed something over two tons, though we did not have an opportunity of determining the exact figure. This weight was reflected in the tyre wear, for despite a modest speed of 55 mph on the outward run, both the rear tyres were very badly worn on arrival at Calino, i.e. after about a thousand miles. Subsequent high speed runs over some 2000 miles of Italian roads and autostrada proved sufficient to render useless four of the covers in as much as no semblance of tread was left on two of the covers, and very little on the remaining two. For the return journey we fitted two 6.50 x 16 racing covers to Mark VII wheels and put these on the front of the car. Tyre pressures used were 30 lbs. front, 35 lbs. rear in the dry; 27 front, 32 rear in the wet.

Considering the unfavourable weight distribution, the car on the whole handled remarkably well. Most forcible reminder of this weight was a violent oversteer which set in when rounding fast or medium fast bends. This was partially nullified by running the front tyres at a considerably lower pressure than the rears.

JOE SUTTON, former racing mechanic

'I was chief mechanic to Number 20 at Le Mans in 1951, and my two drivers were Peter Walker and Peter Whitehead. The whole thing was done on a shoestring, because my mechanic was either one of the two drivers, depending who was free at the time. So if Peter Whitehead came in, he was my mechanic till Peter Walker took over. That's how it worked.

'The other cars had broken oil pipes but mine kept going and I was fortunate, the first time, to be the mechanic to the winning car at Le Mans – just a lucky break.'

'I was coming back through customs on one occasion with a C-type and I'd got through and was nattering with this customs bloke about cars. Old Peter Walker comes out as large as life and says, "Ah, I'm glad you got out. Did they find the watches?".

'I said, "No, we got them hidden too well, Peter!"

'Of course, the customs bloke knew that was one thing we would never do.'

'One year Mike Hawthorn had done the fastest lap at Reims and the prize was 75 bottles of Champagne. So he asked us to bring them back. He told us to take the two cases of 25 for him and to share the other one between us. So we had a couple of bottles apiece.

'We got to customs and the chap told me to open the van.

' "Anything you want to see?" I asked.

' "Yes," he said, "I want to see these two cases of Champagne you've got!"

'In 1954, I think it was, Ted Brookes and myself were mechanics to Ecurie Belge at Le Mans. They were using some foreign tyres and about every two laps the treads blew off.

'Ted had been their mechanic before. Anyway they'd just done a pit stop and Ted said, "Come on. We'll go round the back and have a smoke. They won't want us for a bit now."

From left to right, we see Joe Sutton, Norman Dewis and Frank Rainbow in front of the mobile timekeeper's vehicle at Jabbeke. (Frank Rainbow)

'We'd only been out the back a few minutes, when suddenly there were shouts of "mechanicians, ici, quick!"'

'Instead of us coming through the pit and over the counter, we came through a trade pit which had got no counter at all. Ted and I took one look and saw what had happened. We got the car jacked up, the wheels changed and the car going out and they're still shouting, "Jagwah mechanicians".'

'Ted and I were leaning on the counter, and when they looked round there was complete astonishment. They didn't even know the car had gone!

'As I said, the whole thing was done on a shoestring, and we didn't get paid a lot. We only got two hours overtime a day when we were at Le Mans. No matter how long you worked, you only got paid for two.

'This happened after Le Mans in '51 because we put a helluva sheet in for overtime, because we'd done plenty.

'Thurstans, the accountant at Jaguar – do you know what he said to one of the other mechanics, Jack Lea? He said, "You've had the pleasure of going".

'The mechanic replied, "Yes, we've had the pleasure of going to work. The mere fact that we won is incidental. That's due to our efforts." '

FRANK RAINBOW, riding and racing mechanic,

and member of the Engine Development Department, on the 1950 Tourist Trophy which a young Stirling Moss won in an XK120.
'I have never seen it rain so much in all my life. But it was hilarious. On the opposite side of the road to the pits was a beer tent.

'All the good souls were watching the racing with pints in their hands – Guinness and so forth. The rain came down and the wind blew. Then, all of a sudden, this marquee just collapsed!

'It was the funniest thing in the world to see people clambering out, and still clutching their pints!

'We weren't too badly off in the pits, but they were a bit primitive. They'd got tarpaulins over the top on some sort of scaffolding. Every so often the tarpaulin would fill up with rain, and then the wind would blow it over us standing in front of the pits. But it was a very interesting race.

'Moss had the capability of being able to assess a corner probably better than anyone else. Often he didn't have the power that some of the others had, but he could still do a faster lap.

'He had his twenty-first birthday there and he said, "Look at my hair. It's disappearing already. My old man's got three dentist's surgeries, he's got all these chemist pals, and none of them can give me anything to make my hair grow!"

'Probably about three o' clock in the afternoon, Mr Hassan would come along and say, "You'd better take a car and pick-up young John [Lyons] from school".

'I used to buy John an ice cream, because he didn't seem to have any pocket money of his own.

'After his apprenticeship at Leyland, he came to the factory and he was working alongside me in our department for some weeks. He was making a tour of the works, seeing how everything went.'

Meteor contract: Mr. Lyons reported that we had received notification from the Ministry of Supply that production of the Meteor engine was to be drastically reduced and under the circumstances we shall not be called upon to go into production beyond an initial quantity for trial purposes.

Browns Lane: Mr. Lyons reported that we are well established in the new factory. The paint shop was operating as satisfactorily as we could hope.

Negotiations were going on with the Pressed Steel Company for the production of a pressed steel body for a new 2-litre car which we had in hand, and which it was hoped we should be able to sell for a price not exceeding £695 excluding Purchase Tax.

The name of Soapy Sutton is a well known one in Jaguar history. He did most of the road testing in the late forties and early fifties, and is particularly remembered for driving the XK120 at Jabbeke. I have often wondered why he was called Soapy and asked Frank.

'I gathered why Ron Sutton was called "Soapy" from Harold Irving. He was the Chairman of Champion Sparking Plugs, but had been mechanic to Sir Henry Segrave's *Golden Arrow* when it broke the World Land Speed Record.

'They went to some event in France and every morning Ron always got soap in his ears after he'd had a wash. So they called him "Soapy", and the name stuck – just like a lot of school kids!'

––––––––––

The year 1953 was, of course, a disastrous one for Jaguar and the long nose C-Types all overheated with dire results. As some of the plumbing work had been carried out by a Roy Kettle, though he was not to blame for the problems, these cars were nicknamed the "Kettle Specials"!

'We'd got this water leak and our car was the only one still going. The two others had already fallen out. Jack Emerson, who was in charge of the engine side, told me to put some water in, so I did.

'He said, "I think that's enough, Frank".

'I said, "Why?" He was standing by those short exhaust pipes.

"Well," he said, "I've got my shoes full already!"

––––––––––

'It would be during a race in 1953 that John Bolster was bending down over a car with his microphone during a pitstop, and I was changing a wheel. The hammer slipped straight out of my hand, and went straight between his legs!

'So he had to do a hop, skip and a jump!'

––––––––––––

Taken from Norman Dewis's log entitled 'BRONCO 1'
This is the strange device designed by Sir William that was nicknamed
the *Brontosaurus*.

Axle: Salisbury 3.31:1 (see below)
Brakes: Lockheed 2 L-S
Brake Fluid: Lockheed Green
Rack and pinion steering
Enveloping body
Enclosed wheels
Works Order No. WCR 1148

19.09.53	Car prepared for drag tests at Gaydon.
20.09.53	Drag tests made at Gaydon with and without front blanking plates. 15% approx. better than XK120C.
23.09.53	4.09:1 axle removed and Salisbury 3.31:1 fitted. Filled with $3^1/2$ pints of lead soap additive No. S 2497 Speedo changed to ATS 505.
28.09.53	Tests at Lindley. 1st test – speedo correction.

Speedo:- 30   50   70   90   110
Actual:-   30 $49^1/2$ $68^1/2$ 87   107

2nd test – tyre temperatures. Tyre size:- 6.50 x 16 all round.
Tyre pressures:- 30 lbs front, 35 lbs rear.
Dunlop rep. Mr. Simmonds. Air temp:- 54 degrees F.

Tyre temp:-	N-F	N-R	O-R	O-F
15 mins.	47	48	47	47 degrees C.

Water temp:-   60 degrees C.
Oil pressure:- 40 lbs.

BOARD MEETING
JULY, 1953

Mr. Lyons reported that production was satisfactory and as a matter of fact the schedule of output had been increased to some 250 cars per week, and although this figure had on occasions been attained, the general output was running at about 230 cars per week. In view of the general dissatisfaction expressed by the Home distributors as to the number of cars released to the Home market, it was intended to step up quantities released to them which could now be done without detriment to our export requirements, which would still average about 70% of the output.

In the fifties a television programme, probably Sportsview, set up a competition in the studio between the Jaguar and Aston Martin mechanics. The contest consisted of changing wheels and plugs and, obviously, the winners were the team who completed the operation first.

The Jaguar team won easily.

How did they do it? Simple. They had machined all but a single thread off the spinners and spark plugs!

Test cancelled owing to the O-F wing valance shaking loose and falling off the car. Both front wing valances will have to be fitted more securely.

Maximum rpm obtained at Lindley – 5200 rpm

29.09.53   Car weight 21 cwt.
H.P. required:-

10 mph	1.035 hp
20 mph	2.36 hp
30 mph	4.2 hp
40 mph	6.94 hp
50 mph	10.7 hp
60 mph	15.78 hp
70 mph	22.98 hp
80 mph	30.9 hp
90 mph	43.5 hp
100 mph	57.8 hp

30.09.53   Front and rear wing valances being made secure by fitting dzeus fasteners.

PHIL WEAVER, who for many years ran the Competition Shop

'Most of the XK engine development was done by Jack Emerson. Jack was a very clever bloke. He was one of these silent people. He didn't say much but what he did say was good.

'The XK engine, in its highly tuned form, was rather unkind to cylinder head gaskets. When you were racing it, it used to blow water out of the gasket. The gasket hadn't got sufficient land on it to seal it. The expansion rates between the alloy head and iron block were, of course, different.

'Because of this differential expansion, which everybody gets, it is easy to overstress the cylinder head stud. When we were racing, we weren't absolutely trouble free – don't think that for one minute. Although we won races, it was because of the slick work of the mechanics, there's no two ways about it. We used to use a lot of water. It used to blow water out of the gasket. But Jack solved it, quite simply.

'He used a thread of cotton. Last thing, before the cylinder head on all our racing engines was dropped on to the block, Jack used to put a continuous piece of cotton right the way around the studs and just overlap it, and then drop the head down on it. That completely cured it!

'Old Jack actually cured that without any big modification. He'd learnt all these wrinkles in his motor cycling days. A very sound engineer, Jack was.

'He first did that in the XK120 days and it carried on right the way through. He also used to do it on any customer engines, like those for Brian Lister, Ecurie Ecosse, and people like that.'

'You've heard of the Brontosaurus. Well, a lot used to go on between the right way to do things and the wrong way to do things. The Old Man had his way of doing it with Fred Gardner. Although old Fred was a woodworking man, he and the Old Man used to get in the Body Shop, as it was then, and cook things up themselves. Old Fred actually had enough skilled personnel, not only in woodworking, but also in panel making and welding, that they could conjure up something unbeknown to Mr Heynes.

'I well remember the Old Man coming up to me and saying, "Weaver, I want that to run". So I had to go into the Body Shop, old

Fred Gardner's holy of holies, and there was this monstrous looking thing, stuck there.

'We had to work all hours, night and day, to fix D-type bits on it so as to get it to run round the works. He wanted it done in five minutes!'

The emphatic victory at Le Mans in 1953 received the approval of Her Majesty The Queen. (Jaguar Cars)

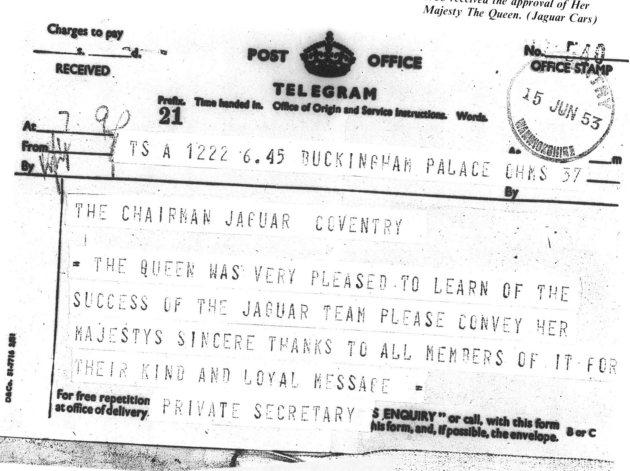

A small booklet was prepared to aid communication at Le Mans in 1953.

The Jaguar D-type even had a sales brochure. It seems rather amazing that Jaguar should go to the trouble, or even feel that they needed to produce such a publication, for a hand-built sports-racing car.

The J A G U A R 'D' Type

S P E C I F I C A T I O N

ENGINE. Six cylinder 3½ litre Jaguar engine 83 mm., 106 mm., 3,442 c.c. Twin overhead camshafts driven by two stage chain. Cylinder head of high tensile aluminium alloy with hemi-spherical combustion chambers. Aluminium alloy pistons, steel connecting rods. Forced lubrication on dry sump principle. Cooling by pump.

TRANSMISSION. 4 speed synchromesh gearbox operated by central remote control lever. Triple dry plate clutch.

SUSPENSION. Independent front suspension incorporating transverse wishbones and torsion bars with telescopic shock absorbers. Rear suspension by trailing links and torsion bar with telescopic shock absorbers.

BRAKES. Dunlop disc type.

STEERING. Rack and pinion. Steering wheel adjustable for reach.

WHEELS AND TYRES. Dunlop light alloy perforated disc with centre lock hubs. Dunlop Racing tyres and tubes.

FUEL SUPPLY. By large S.U. electric pumps from rear mounted tanks.

ELECTRICAL EQUIPMENT. 12v. 40 amp-hour battery. Constant voltage controlled ventilated dynamo. Flush fitting headlamps and sidelamps, integral stop/tail lamps with built-in reflectors. Instrument panel light. Horn. Starter motor.

INSTRUMENTS. Revolution counter, oil pressure gauge, water thermometer gauge, ignition warning light.

FRAME AND BODY. Integral frame and body. Body of light alloy, constructed on monocoque principles. Two seater body complying with F.I.A. sports car regulations. Spare wheel carried horizontally in tail.

DIMENSIONS. Overall length 14' 8", overall width 5' 4½'. Height at scuttle 2' 8", wheelbase 7' 6". Track (front) 4' 2", (rear) 4'.

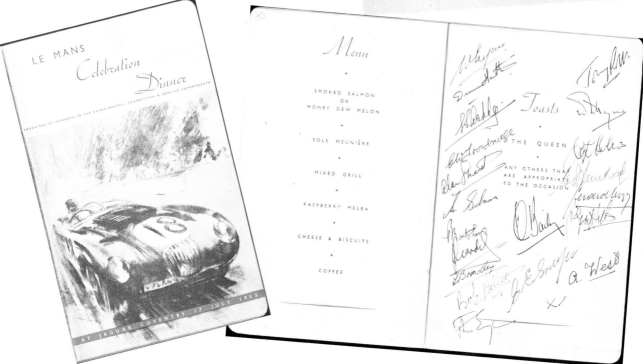

S.S. 90 – Almost concours condition. High compression head, excellent performance. £185. Terms.

February 1955

Reconditioned S.S.100 3¹/2-litre drophead coupe. This rare specimen is probably the only one in existence, being the 1939 show model. It has the main characteristics of the 100 with the flared wings but is fitted with attractive drophead bodywork complete with winding windows. Fold flat screen, large dials, remote control, etc. Space for luggage or uncomfortable third passenger. Just released from the bodyworks after expert recellulosing in metallescent silver grey to contrast with the deep blue leather upholstery. £325.

March 1955

Ian Appleyard, and his former wife Pat (née Lyons), with the 1953 Monte Carlo Mark VII. (Jaguar Cars)

From an unknown US publication dated 1954.

"Imagine, Mrs. Willard said her husband bought one for pleasure riding!"

Nov.-Dec. 1954

INTER-DEPARTMENTAL COMMUNICATION – JAGUAR
CARS 1953

PRIZE AND BONUS MONEY – LE MANS

	1st	2nd	4th	TEAM & CLASS, ETC		TOTAL
GENERAL CATEGORY	*1st*	*2nd*	*4th*			
INDEX OF PERFORMANCE	*4th*	*5th*	*7th*			
Prize Money	£2200	£706	£125			£3031
Lucas	75	50				125
Champion	100	50		T.30	C.10	190
Girlings	30	20				50
Dunlop	250	150		T.50		450
Shell	100	–		T.100		200
Mintex	60	30			C.10	100
Totals:-	£2815	£1006	£125	£200		£4146

*Also due to the Drivers in respect of Starting Money and Retaining Fees.
(Due 1st July).*

	Retaining Fee	Starting Money	Total
Stirling Moss	–	–	
P.D.C. Walker	200	100	300
A.P.R. Rolt	200	100	300
J.M. Stewart	100	100	200
J.D. Hamilton	100	100	200
P.N. Whitehead	100	100	200
Totals:-	£700	£500	£1200

This is a well known shot of the Brontosaurus but it serves to show what an extraordinary monster it was. On the other hand, the spats pre-dated the XJR-6 by around 30 years! (Jaguar Cars)

The XK120 (middle row, far right)
and its competition in the fifties.

Lofty England seen at his desk in the fifties.

S.S.I Airliner Saloon, 20 hp, VGC. £65 ono.

January 1958

S.S.I Sports 4-seater, unusually well cared for, B.R.G. Beautiful engine, recent steering and brake overhaul. Zip tonneau. £89.

February 1958

Not surprisingly, firms were keen to align themselves with Jaguar's successes and the English Steel Corporation used this splendid photo and caption in their booklet on Torsion Bars.

SILVERSTONE 1955. Photograph shows Mike Hawthorn, leader of the Jaguar team, in action with the " D " type Jaguar fitted with E.S.C. Torsion Bars. During this race Hawthorn set up a new sports car lap record of 95·79 m.p.h.

Introduction

A torsion bar is a very simple type of spring, and, as the name implies, consists merely of a bar which is gripped at each end and twisted. This twist provides the springing.

The ordinary coil-spring is simply a torsion bar which has been coiled into helical form.

The section of the bar is usually circular, although other sections, i.e. square and rectangular, can be used. The circular section bar, however, is the most economical on space and weight, since it will absorb the highest energy per unit of weight and is also the easiest design to produce commercially.

In its simplest form it looks like this:—

The heads may be serrated as shown, or have a polygonal section, usually hexagonal or octagonal, although square ends have been made. In addition there may be spigots at the ends for locating the bar.

Some variants on the basic design are shown below:—

1

COMPANY CARS 31 AUGUST 1953

MARK VII SALOONS
LDU 268   710136   Grey   Mr. Lyons
ODU 849   716438 D.N.   Black   Mr. Lyons (De Normanville Overdrive)
MRW 768   713438   Black   Chauffeur
Mk. VII
No. 1   710001   (Service School Chassis)
U.S.A. 1. 735556 BW   Mr. Eerdmans America
U.S.A. 2. 736391 BW   Mr. Reid America
U.S.A. 3. 735189 BW   Mr. Hickman America
U.S.A. 4. 732338   Mr. B. Smith America
XK120 OPEN 2 SEATERS
XK. No. 3 661078   White.   (Distributors Show Car)
MDU 524   660986   Green.   Press Car.
MARK VI SALOON
HRW 488   620004   Black (XK Engine) (J. Flattery)
MARK V SALOONS
MRW 487   620006   Birch Grey.   Meteor Contract Ferry
JRW 393   622222   Black.   Service Chauffeur
JRW 422   621852   Black.   F. Ford
JRW 416   621944   Black.   E. Warren
1946 1¹/₂ LITRE SALOON
HWK 252   410001   Black.   Spares Dept.
NOTE:
The original HRW 488 – 620004 has been broken up and the registration
number and chassis number transferred to Mark VI chassis 623173 Ex.
Experimental Department.

HRW 487 – 620006 and Mark IX Saloon (Ex. Lockheed) have been made
into one good car and registered HRW 487.

XK 2 LITRE
No. 1   470001   Prototype
XK SPECIAL MODELS
XK 120 C. Light Alloy Body
XK Special with enclosed wheels (Bronco)

Mark III (1948 type Saloon Body and XJ Chassis)
CDU 700 1937 S.S. Saloon
CDU 431 Vauxhall Velox
Studebaker Champion G.297326
NOTE:
XK 120 C – XKC.001 – Dismantled and parts passed to Service Dept.
669001 White Fixed Head Coupe fitted with 2 Litre Engine has been
dismantled.
710229 has changed identity with 710004. KRW 621 and original white
710004 has been broken down for salvage.
Prototype Mark IV XK 120 F.H.C. has adopted Chassis No. 660001.
HKV 455 and original Blue 660001 Open 2 Seater is to be broken up.

During 1954 the D-type, XKD 406, was taken to Silverstone for various drivers to try.

Jimmy Stewart put in 12 laps in the wet and recorded a best of 2.11. With the wet surface drying, he put in a further 15 laps with a best of 2.5. In fact, he showed remarkable consis-tency recording that time on no less than 9 of his 12 flying laps.

With the surface semi-dry, Ninian Sanderson achieved 2.03 during his 10 laps, Peter Walker then posted a 1.57 amongst his 23 laps and Bob Berry clocked up 21 laps. On his penultimate lap he stopped the clock at 1.54.5.

**Extract from booklet produced
by ENGLISH STEEL FORGE
AND ENGINEERING
CORPORATION**

'A torsion bar is a very simple type of spring, and, as the name implies, consists merely of a bar which is gripped at each end and twisted. This twist provides the springing.

'The ordinary coil spring is simply a torsion bar which has been coiled into helical form.

'The section of the bar is usually circular, although other sections, i.e. square and rectangular, can be used. The circular section bar, however, is the most economical on space and weight, since it will absorb the highest energy per unit of weight and is also the easiest design to produce commer-cially.

'The heads may be serrated, or have a polygonal section, usually hexa-gonal or octagonal, although square ends have been made. In addition there may be spigots at the end for locating the bar.

'The largest single use of torsion bars has been motor-car suspensions. The torsion bar has some advantages over the helical spring for both independent front and rear wheel sus-pension because of its great compact-ness of design, and its greater load-carrying capacity which means that the unsprung weight of the vehicle is reduced. They are also used for sus-pension of very heavy vehicles such as tanks or other armoured fighting vehi-cles, passenger buses, railway coaches, lorries, etc.

'An interesting variation on the principle is that of anti-roll bars for motor cars. This consists of a torsion bar bent near the ends. and with a forged eye in place of the normal splined head.'

Alice Fenton was a remarkable lady who joined the fledgling Swallow company in the early days in Blackpool and rose through the ranks to become the Home Sales Director. (Jaguar Cars)

Right: E.W. 'Bill' Rankin was the man who created so much of the Jaguar image in conjunction with Jaguar's advertising agency. (Jaguar Cars)

This is a shot of Hoffman's showrooms in Park Avenue, New York, but it is a curious one. I have seen 'exactly' the same photograph, but with a different car in it. If you look closely, you will see that the car has been superimposed upon the photo and is, in fact, grossly out of scale with the car behind – and he's parked a bit close!

LES BOTTRILL, member of the Competition Department until moving to the US as a service engineer

'I started in 1950, and then in 1954 I was transferred into the Competition Department, where they built all the Production D-types, the few that were built. I track tested every single one of those, and some of the Works cars.

'We did most of the test work at MIRA although we drove them on the road as well. I used to do about 300 or 400 miles on each car. just to run everything in. Interjected with that we used to do a little tyre testing for Dunlops. Norman Dewis used to do most of the experimental test work, but it was all a lot of fun.

'We had a couple of near misses, but nothing serious. At MIRA, if you were going to run above 100 mph average, they used to restrict the amount of vehicles on the banked circuit, and you had to run above the yellow line on the outside. I was going round one day and saw this Land Rover. MIRA used to be an old RAF base, or whatever, so up to the circuit in various spots were aprons and bits of runway. I saw this guy in various spots and he'd got people taking photographs.

'I was a little worried by this because he was very close up by the circuit, then he'd disappear. A few minutes later I saw him on the end of one of the banks, and he was right on the edge of the safety wire. I had a thought in my head. "He's gonna move," and he sure did. He came onto the circuit.

' "What am I goin to do now?" I thought. "Back side of him, front side of him?" Anyway I went off into the infield, missed everything fortunately, didn't do any damage, didn't flip or anything. Then he just disappeared. That was a little scary!

'Then one other day – it was in the early part of the winter, I suppose, and it was frosty – I'd been running round and the track started to get a little ice on it. I pulled in and thought that was enough for the day.

'Then I saw Ken Richardson, who used to be the Chief Tester for Triumph, go out in a TR2 or TR3 and started barrelling round. Just the north bank was in the shade and that was the one that had got ice on it. I'd found it awfully slippery the last time round, and I thought if he goes into that full belt, he's goin . . .

'So I went off again and chased him round to flag him down. He thought I was racing him. But I managed to pull in front of him and slowed him down.

'Those were a couple of incidents I had with the D-types. You'd hit a couple of crows occasionally and they gave you a good whack. I hit one one day and it punched quite a big dent in the front. I couldn't do anything about it. You wouldn't believe the shock you get through the car if you hit a crow at 140/150 mph.

'Depending on the gearing, I guess a stock 'D' could run up to about 145 on the back straight. When they first came out with the fuel restrictions at Le Mans, I did a test run on one test car to see how hard we could run it with the mixture as lean as possible. I think I did about 144 miles in the hour. You could do about 170 on the back stretch in the Works cars!'

RONNIE ADAMS, on the Monte Carlo Rally

'The Jaguar factory took more interest in 1953 when Ian Appleyard and Cecil Vard took second and fourth places in works cars followed by myself in fifteenth place with my privately-owned Mark VII.

'Appleyard did not compete in 1954, but myself and Vard took sixth and eighth places being unlucky not to win the Charles Faroux Team Trophy due to the third member of our nominated team only reaching

BOARD MEETING FRIDAY 9 JULY 1954

Henlys Limited: Mr. Lyons reported that Henlys had signed a lease for new showrooms in Piccadilly for a period of 42 years. The showroom would be solely devoted to Jaguar cars. It has been agreed that this Company will contribute £5000 per annum towards the expenses of this showroom and will also pay one-third of the cost of shop front decorations, which will cost approximately £20,000. It is agreed that the whole of the ground floor will be staffed by Messrs. Henlys Limited with salesmen selling only Jaguar cars and that they use the basement and the first floor for the sale and display of used cars.

TED BROOKES, former racing mechanic and Superintendent of the Experimental Shop, on the great rivalry, both on the track and off, between those two great gentlemen and sportsmen, Tommy Sopwith and John Coombs.

'There was an occasion when I delivered a special Mark II to John Coombs, in the evening. I arrived at Guildford about seven o'clock and Tom hadn't had his car. They were both having one at the same time, but Tom hadn't actually got his yet.

'When I got to Guildford, the first thing that John Coombs asked me was, "has Tommy Sopwith had his car yet?"

I said, "No".

"Right," he said, "I'll run you back to the station at Euston."

'We toured London, trying to find Tommy Sopwith! We went to the Steering Wheel Club and all the pubs he could think of, before we got to the station. We couldn't find him, but the object was to show off his car!'

156th place. I came near to an outright win by leading the Rally on arrival at Monte Carlo, only being beaten on handicap by the small cars on the Monaco circuit.

'1955 saw the first full works team of Mark VIIs driven by myself, Vard and Appleyard, finishing 8th, 27th and 84th respectively. That year saw the beginning of Vard's run of bad luck when he was heavily penalised at a newly innovated secret control. Appleyard suffered even worse luck when a core plug of his cylinder block dropped out forcing his retirement during the Mountain Circuit Test. An amazing photograph appeared in a motoring journal of Appleyard's car – with steam rising to the mountain tops – which had been taken from my car when waiting to check in at a Control. Nevertheless we did win the Charles Faroux Trophy.

'In 1956 the works team consisted of myself, Vard and Reg Mansbridge (Appleyard again not competing). I gained an outright win followed by Mansbridge in 45th and Vard in 153rd place, the latter having been unluckily involved in a collision with a non-competing car which put paid to our chances of the team prize.'

RONNIE ADAMS

The Chequered Flag (London) Ltd, offer: C-type, ex-Ecurie Ecosse, D-type mods, suitable as road or track car, finished in BRG, full weather equipment. £965.

1938   3¹/₂-litre   SS100.   Excellent throughout. New weather equipment, tyres, etc. £285 or offers. Must sell. HP arranged.

July 1960

What you might, perhaps, call an 'inaction shot'!

In June, 1957 Bill Heynes put together his 'Notes on Suggested Models for 1958'. The following are extracts taken from those notes

A trifle over-the-top, perhaps, this XK120 Fixed-Head. (Jaguar Cars)

Mark VIII
To the best of my knowledge no major changes are envisaged on this model. If changes are required the following would be suggested:-

1)   Adjustable Front Bucket Seats now offered as optional.
2)   Adjustable Bench Seats. This in my opinion is most desirable as I personally find the bench seat quite a strain to drive on a long journey.
3)   Adjustable Rear Seats. I understand that these are supplied as an optional feature on the Humber Hawk and I believe it would be quite a selling feature on the Mark VIII.
6)   Disc Brakes. If it is essential, it is felt that the present disc as used on the XK150 can be employed. We should, of course, be liable to get criticism on the basis of excessive wear if the brakes were deliberately abused, but this would only be in a small percentage of cases. It is felt that for fade and performance the brake is probably at least equivalent to the existing Girling drum brake and that we need have no qualms in this respect.

Whilst on the question of drum brakes it has come to light that a certain amount of trouble has been experienced on the TR.3 with the disc brakes under severe icing conditions where the car has either been allowed to stand in driving snow or has been driven in driving snow without use of the brakes. I have no direct information that this has actually happened, although both Dunlop and Girling are fairly keyed up on this possibility at the moment.

The obvious solution, of course, is to fit a drum transmission brake which would also act as a handbrake instead of having the handbrake on the rear discs, and it is probably the most satisfactory solution that can be devised.

2.4 'S' TYPE
1) Blue head S.U. carburettors.
2) $3/8''$ lift camshafts.
3) Suction tank for brake servo necessary due to the low suction at the bottom end.
4) Disc brakes – standard.
5) Wire wheels – standard.
6) 3.4 Radiator aperture necessary due to the increased horse-power output of this engine.
7) 60 watt headlamps – standard.

JAGUAR - VOLKSWAGEN - PORSCHE - JAVELIN-JUPITER
SIMCA - ASTON-MARTIN - LAGONDA

THE HOFFMAN MOTOR CAR CO., INC.

M. E. HOFFMAN
PRESIDENT

487 PARK AVENUE
NEW YORK 22, N. Y.
PLAZA 9-7036-7-8

Max Hoffman's business card.

10 RICHARD HASSAN, Ex-Jaguar apprentice and son of Walter

'Back in the fifties, Bill and Dutch Heynes got the caravan bug and came down to Saundersfoot, where we kept ours, one summer. They came down for a fortnight, and we were all on the same field.

'Then they used to come down at weekends, and on Sunday night Bill and dad would go back to Coventry – Bill to Jaguar, dad to Coventry Climax. One weekend he said, "I am going to bring a new prototype down next weekend, it should be ready. In fact, I've asked for it to be made ready.

'He came down on the Friday night, very late, in the first of the 2.4 Mark I prototypes. It was painted, but it was very bare, with very little chrome. There was a radiator on it, but no badge or anything like that.

'My father had a boat over on the Haven and at that time a Mark VII. So the whole crowd of us got into the two cars and off we went to have a picnic. One of my brothers and I asked if we could have a go in the new "Jag". Mr Heynes loved children and readily agreed.

'It was decided my father would go ahead with all the gear and get the boat near the steps, and Bill Heynes would take my mum and Mrs. Heynes and us kids through Haverfordwest to get some more food for the picnic.

'So Bill Heynes drove into the centre of Haverfordwest, which you could do in those days, and parked smack in the middle of the High Street, outside one of the shops. We noticed a policeman looking at the car, and he wandered over.

'The policeman put his head through the window and said, "What's this then?"

'Mr Heynes very bravely said, "I am not allowed to tell you". This is to a uniformed policeman!

' "Oh," he said, "Is it one of those secret new models, is it?"

' "I am afraid I can't . . .

' "Looks like a special-bodied Alvis to me!"

' "Possibly."

'He then walked all round it, and walked off!'

'Did that car rock and roll. It had tremendous roll. It is quite a fast road back from Haverfordwest to Tenby and my father could drive quite briskly if he wanted to. He proceeded to do so and Bill Heynes had to try and keep up with him. This old thing was coming round the bends on the door handles!'

On the integral construction Mark VII

'That was a lovely car. It was the first monocoque saloon that they did. It had XK140 running gear and was very low. You could tell how low it was because it used a little 140 gear stick. Externally it had Mark VII panels, with a single piece windscreen and wire wheels.

'I used to look at that car, as a youngster, and I thought, "I wonder if one day they'll sell it". They cut it up. Very important car that, really, because, other than the wartime thing that dad built, that was their first integral monocoque saloon.

On the VA and VB Jeeps built by his father during the war

'These were two totally different vehicles. The one had a little Jap air-cooled engine and the other one had a Ford 8 or 10 engine.

'The VB used sheets of steel, corrugated and the whole lot welded together. That gave it a very simple box construction. But it had very clever suspension on it, rather like Chapman had in the end and which he christened as his strut. It had an identical rear suspension to that with a pump housing with a coil spring straight up to the top coil, and used the half-shaft as its outrigger. It had to be built very light.

'My father used it as a road car during the war. We used to go down to London in it on odd weekends, because he had petrol rations for development. We'd all jump in the back and off we'd go. It was like a very small jeep and ended up at Farnborough because it was paid for by the Ministry of Defence.

On the glass-fibre D-type, which it has often been stated never existed

'Oh, it did because we had it on show in Coventry with Mike Hawthorn one day. He came up to make the "Ernie" Premium Bonds selection. They had a big procession in Coventry during the week and Mike Hawthorn was the celebrity who pressed the button.

'It was done in Owen Owens, the store in the centre. The only "D" we could lay our hands on that morning was the fibre glass one.

'It ran round Coventry that morning.'

It has often been stated that the car was built by the apprentices.

'No. It was built in Competition and in a fibre-glass shop next to the laboratory. A chap called Thompson ran that section, and he used to do all the fibre glass panels.

'All the external parts were fibre-glass but it had a steel frame. I don't remember too much about the detail, but I am sure those panels ended up on a Ford 10 Special, which this chap Thompson built. He kept the panels. When it was cut up, he just removed all the panels.

'There was one 3.8 we had in Experimental which got written off. Richard Soames wrote it off when he hit the local chimney sweep up in Wales. Can you imagine the big cloud of black dust going up? The sweep was driving an A35 van, and it was like an atom bomb going off as he hit it broadside on!'

Jaguar could hardly have dreamt that, thanks to Ecurie Ecosse, the D-type would take a third Le Mans win after the company had retired from racing.

No matter to whom you speak amongst the former Jaguar men, their favourite driver was always Mike Hawthorn, who enjoyed one of his great duels with Fangio in a D-type at Le Mans in 1955.
(Jaguar Cars)

Left and
panel, i

This looks curiously reminiscent of the XJ-S in certain areas. It is a special-bodied Fiat built by Farina in 1955.

Messrs.

JAGUAR CARS LTD.

COVENTRY   (Inghilterra)

E·W

EDOARDO WEBER
FABBRICA ITALIANA CARBURATORI
SOCIETÀ PER AZIONI · SEDE LEGALE IN MILANO · CAPITALE L. 100.000.000 VERSATO

DIREZIONE AMMINISTRATIVA: MILANO
VIA GIULINI, 3 - TEL. 89307-86325

TELEGRAMMI: WEBER - BOLOGNA
"   WEBER · MILANO · VIA GIULINI 3
CASELLA POSTALE N. 299 · BOLOGNA
C. C. I. A. BOLOGNA 49709
C. C. I. A. MILANO 349433

| VS. RIFERIMENTO | VS. LETTERA DEL | NS. RIFERIMENTO | DATA |
| WMH/MR.10035 | 26th July, 19 | Uff.Vend. UD/IB | 5th August, 1955 |

Dear Sirs,

Re. your letter of July 26th, 1955.

In answer to your query, we beg to inform that we can supply, for experimental purposes, and for delivery on the first days of September:

3 CARBURETTORS, OUR TYPE 58 DCOA3

with a tuning established in an approximate way, and accompanied with 18 chokes TS 1133a 6/40-42-46. We shall not send any main jets, slow-running jets, pump jets, etc., as they are of the same type as those used for our 45 DCO3 units, of which you already dispose of a sufficient provision.

Here enclosed please find an overall drawing of the carburettor in question, showing the shape and size of the flange, and the center distance between the intake pipes.

Our 58 DCOA3 carburettors can be supplied at the price of Lit. 60.000,-- each, for goods delivered free at our Works in Bologna. The price of these carburettors is rather high due to their being of an experimental type, of which only a few specimen have been manufactured with no equipment.

The chokes will be invoiced at the price of Lit. 950,-- each.

Other supply conditions: usual, in force between our two Firms.

Yours faithfully,

EDOARDO WEBER
FABBRICA ITALIANA CARBURATORI
IL DIRETTORE
(F. Micardi)

Mod. 9/c/6 UNI A 4 (210×297)

Jaguar never adopted Weber carburettors on their mass production cars but used them to good effect in racing before the advent of petrol injection.

Grand Prix Jaguars

On several occasions Jaguar's thoughts turned to building a single-seater Grand Prix car. It has been chronicled that two C-type chassis were chopped in half and the two fronts welded together.

Malcolm Sayer, the legendary Jaguar aerodynamicist, actually went so far as to examine and assess various body shapes for such a car and sent a highly secret report to Bill Heynes on 14 May 1956.

WIND-TUNNEL TESTS ON SINGLE SEATER

1) EQUIPMENT USED.

A single-seater model (Diag. 1) was made, containing two electric motors to drive the road wheels, which had tread patterns, lightening holes, etc. as near to reality as practicable. The electric motors were connected to variable resistances, so speeds of wheel rotation were adjustable by stroboscope to match speeds of airflow. The model had a normal Grand Prix type body, but of good aerodynamic form, and with outlets for radiator air formed by front suspension fairings.

2) DRAG OF CAR.

This proved to be 126% of the 1955 D-type, i.e. on 250 b.h.p. maximum speed would be 182 m.p.h. compared with 197 m.p.h. for the D-type.

JOHN COOMBS, for many years one of the main Jaguar dealers and famous entrant of Mark IIs and E-types, amongst others. His drivers included Roy Salvadori, Graham Hill and Jackie Stewart.

'After Graham and Roy had left, I was then left with having to have various other drivers. Bob Jane came along, and we had Colin Chapman. He was remarkably quick. Jack Sears, who was no mean driver, was seen off by Colin Chapman in his first race in a 3.8, which was really remarkable.

'I suppose the most exciting race we ever had, looking back to the saloons, was with Roy Salvadori and Stirling Moss. Tommy Sopwith employed Stirling to drive at the International Meeting at Silverstone. In practice Stirling was fractionally quicker than Roy, and one assumed that he was going to win the race.

'Roy said to me on the grid, "This is one that I don't think we are going to win. I don't think I can get past him".

'To my amazement – well, not to my amazement, because Roy was very versatile and could always pull something out of the bag – he passed and repassed Stirling lap after lap. It was the most incredible race. They came through Woodcote side by side, literally flat out, nobody giving.

'Roy won on the last lap. He passed Stirling coming down Hangar Straight, which was fabulous. It was a super race.'

These fascinating illustrations show Malcolm Sayer's thoughts for a Grand Prix Jaguar in 1956. Diag. 2 looks remarkably akin to the all-enveloping Connaught, whereas Diag. 4 is vaguely reminiscent of the Bugatti Type 251 post-war racing car where the nose broadens to guide air around the front wheels. In this area it also reminds one of much more modern single-seater cars and Diag. 7 is obviously similar to the 1954 GP Lancias that were handed over to Ferrari to race.

3) ANALYSIS OF DRAG.

By changing various parts it was possible after many tests to apportion the drag at 180 m.p.h. as follows:-

Main body of car, including driver	46%
Wheels (stationary)	41%
Rotation of wheels	$6^1/2$%
Internal losses (radiator)	$6^1/2$%
Total:	100%

At lower speeds the fact that the wheels are rotating has less effect than that quoted. It will be noticed that it is the aerodynamically bad shape of the wheel rather than its rotation that causes $^7/_8$ of its drag. The flow pattern round a wheel is shown in Diag. 3. The drag of the body was extremely low (18.8 h.p. for 100 m.p.h.) and better than most single-seater aircraft fuselages.

4) REDUCTION OF DRAG.

Numerous ways of nullifying the wheel drag were tried. The results, expressed as percentage reduction in total drag, were as follows:-

a) Fairing in front of wheels (as Gordini & Bugatti) (Diag. 4) .	0
b) Fairing behind wheels (Diag. 5)	$^1/_2$
c) Combination of A & B	$^1/_2$
d) Discs on wheels to improve shape (Diag. 6)	2
e) Lancia-type sponson fairings (Diag. 7)	5
f) Combination of E & A	5
g) As E but solid between body and sponson	1
h) Thin sheet-metal "sponson" (Diag. 8)	5
i) As H but no flow through intake orifice	11
j) Fibre-glass D-type wings (Diag. 2)	21

Test H was to demonstrate what observations of wool-tufts had led to be suspected, i.e. the sponson fairings act, not by virtue of fairing the wheels, but by erecting a barrier so that smooth flow over the car is not disrupted by turbulence from the front wheels.

Test I was to try the effect of using surface-radiators as sponsons and having no conventional radiator intake orifice. As it might be made as light as normal layouts, and is easily controllable by alternative tappings, its decrease in drag is sufficient to warrant consideration. Vulnerability is no greater than that of Lancia and Ferrari fuel tanks.

Test J shows that with D-type wing the car comes down to the same drag as a 1955 D-type as might be expected.

5) STABILITY.

Although the model tested had no inherent vices, i.e. no excessive positive or negative lift on either axle, it was noticeably unsteady at higher speeds, undoubtedly from the turbulent air from the wheels buffeting the body. Whilst not serious, as aerodynamic unbalance would be, it would improve neither comfort nor handling. It was noticeably less in tests 4 E to 4 X, and disappeared completely with the fitting of wings.

6) MISCELLANEOUS.

a) As splashboards are often fitted nowadays, their effect was tried in various shapes. In general they increase the drag of a normal Grand Prix car by about 3%.

b) Extraction of the radiator air through the rear of the front suspension fairings was very strong, and increased with wheel revs.

7) SUMMARY.

Judged entirely from airflow considerations, conventional Grand Prix cars have at least a 15 m.p.h. disadvantage compared with a "D-type" single-seater. Side-sponsons reduce the disadvantage to 12 m.p.h., whilst retaining the better visibility, brake-cooling, and weight-saving. If used as side radiators they reduce the disadvantage further, to 8 m.p.h. less. These figures are for an exceptionally well-shaped car.

M. G. SAYER

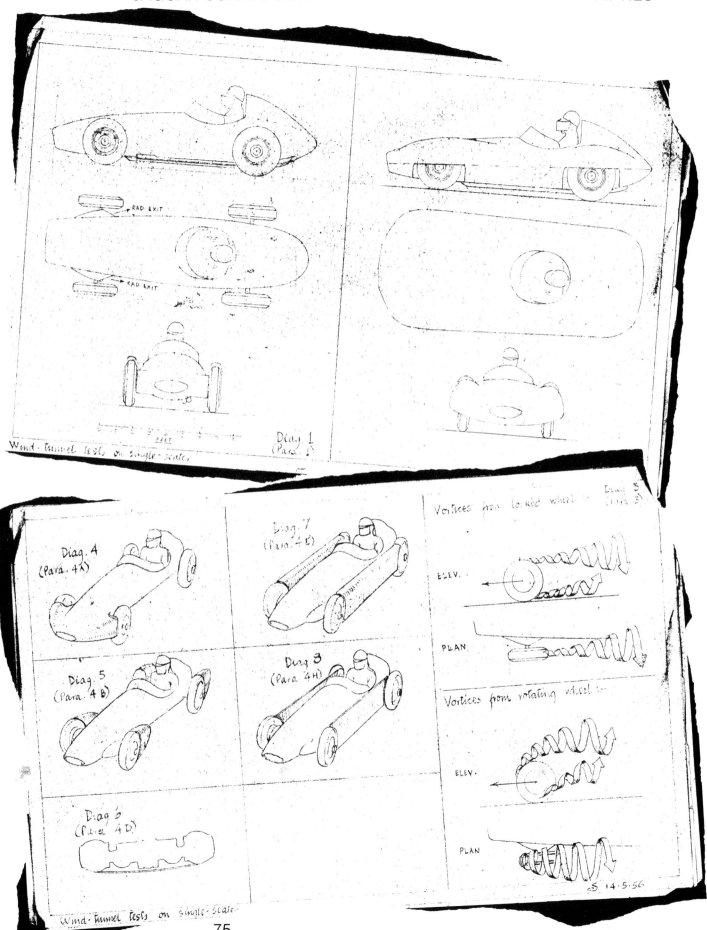

PHIL WEAVER recalls a chassis being built

'It was built of two C-types back to back and it was done on the production line, supervised by Bert Hartshorn in conjunction with us. It never ran though.

'The thing that interfered with it was the factory fire. They set aside the top end of one of the production lines where they were building the C-types, for space to be given to this one.

'Although the Drawing Office gave assistance, where necessary, it was done, sort of, on cigarette packets in the Experimental Machine Shop. Somebody would sketch something out and they'd say, "Oh yes, I like that". And you'd give it to Bill Cassidy, and Bill would make it like that!'

An undated but extremely heavily retouched photograph of the Browns

Lane factory; showing it, perhaps, as the Company would have liked it to look rather than how it actually did look.

TOMMY SOPWITH, who drove saloons before retiring from active competition to run his Equipe Endeavour team. During his racing days he had many famous dices with Mike Hawthorn in Mark Is

'It was great fun racing with someone like Mike Hawthorn because you knew that he wasn't going to make a mistake – of course he was a very much better driver than I was – and therefore you could get very close to him, in perfect confidence.

'I think the biggest compliment I was ever paid in my racing career was after practice at Silverstone. I suppose it was May '58, and Dunlop produced one set of R.5 tyres. Michael said, "you can have them" and Lofty England said "no you can't"!

'I was very pleased about that. Michael had them for the race, and I had them after that. They were the only set. I think that was the biggest compliment I was every paid racing.'

I reminded Tommy Sopwith of the famous occasion when he was dicing and took a rather wider line than usual, and went round the advertising hoardings on the outside of the bend and, continuing at unabated speed, rejoined the circuit proper and recommenced his duel.

'Oh, that was with Michael. That comes of being a spectator. You see I went to school very close to Silverstone, and I actually sat in that stand. So I knew that you could go round the other side and then back again!'

I asked Sopwith why he started his team and called it Equipe Endeavour.

'I suppose the team was started when I was racing. It was fashionable to put "entered by" someone different to you. Gawaine Baillie and I got together, because we were both involved in Woking Motors, and we settled on that name [Tommy's father, the late Sir Thomas Sopwith, had used the name *Endeavour* for his racing yachts. P.P.]. Then when I gave up racing, I ran the team for a few years afterwards and kept the same name going.

'We had the rivalry with Coombs that lasted for quite a long time and which was quite fun.'

This photograph is from Malcolm Sayer's own collection. It shows smoke tunnel tests of a single-seater. Clearly a GP type and rear-engined; the question remains was it a Jaguar project?

Her Majesty The Queen and The Duke of Edinburgh are assisted to the Royal car by Sir William, having completed their famous visit to the factory in 1956.

When asked how many Lister-Jaguar's were made, Brian Lister stated, 'about 20 if we include kits of parts in this country and those exported to the USA'.

It would be interesting to know how many survive – rather more than 20, I fancy!

SIR WILLIAM LYONS

Past President of the Society of Motor Manufacturers and Traders Ltd (1950–51); Past President of the Motor Industry Research Association (1954); Past President of the Motor Trades Benevolent Fund (1954); Appointed Royal Designer for Industry by the Royal Society of Arts in 1954; Created Knight Bachelor 1956.
Recreation: Golf
Private Address: Wappenbury Hall, Leamington Spa, Warwickshire.

On 29 November 1957 the US name of the company was changed from Jaguar Cars North America Corporation to Jaguar Cars Inc.

MR SAMMY NEWSOME, who apart from running the Coventry Theatre became the Coventry dealer, describes his association with the Company (first published in the sixties in the newsletter of the Midland branch of the JDC).

S.H. NEWSOME OF COVENTRY

'The first association of S.H. Newsome and Co. Ltd with Jaguar Cars commenced soon after the old Swallow Coachbuilding Company moved to Coventry from Blackpool. At that time they were specialising in the manufacture of attractive sports bodies on such well known makes as Austin, Wolseley and Standard. As Standard distributors, the company were invited to take up the representation of Swallow bodies on Standard chassis, and thus were one of the earliest firms associated with Swallow bodies for the new Coventry factory.

'When the first S.S. car was produced, we were appointed distributors almost automatically as it was very largely a Standard product, but I must admit that my first impression was not over-enthusiastic. However, we sold a number of this first model but it was not until a year or two later that we began to feel that this new S.S. car really had a future. At that time we were also distributors of MG, Lea-Francis and Riley cars, whose sports cars were long established, and as an enthusiastic racing driver I was perhaps understandably inclined to reserve my interest for those cars which I used for races and competitions. However, the keen and energetic William Lyons persuaded me to drive a 2 1/2-litre S.S. Tourer as a personal car and thereby inspired me with some of his own enthusiasm. Gradually my interest and admiration for the car outweighed my interest in these other makes, so much so that in a year or two I had complaints from both Riley and MG that we were concentrating our energies too much on this new S.S. car for their liking. I was faced with an ultimatum that their representation would be transferred to other dealers unless the S.S. was dropped. This was quite a serious matter to decide upon as for several years past Riley and M.G. cars had provided a substantial part of our turnover. However, careful consideration brought me to the decision that my belief in the future of William Lyons himself, added to the association with our principal agency, Standard Motors, outweighed all other considerations and, albeit reluctantly, I decided to pin my faith to S.S. This was probably one of the most fortunate decisions I have ever made, for not too long afterwards two unforeseen developments took place.

'One was the introduction of the sensational SS Jaguar which established an absolutely new era in high performance cars; the second was the purchase of Riley by Morris Motors. These events took place about five years before the war, and by that time I had increased my interest in Jaguar cars by entering for a number of competitions, such as the R.A.C. Rally and the Scottish Rally, in the original 2½-litre S.S. all of which increased my confidence in the great future which lay ahead for this new and enterprising concern. I was entrusted with a very exciting hotted-up, stripped version of the 2½-litre SS 100 in which I had many exciting runs at Shelsley Walsh and a number of successes culminating in being privileged to drive the first car with the new 3 ½-litre engine. By this time the Jaguar was being taken very seriously as a sports car and putting up splendid performances in all sorts of competitions, all of which helped greatly to establish the marque as a factor to be reckoned with in the industry. Year by year sales increased as a result of the quite phenomenal value represented by these cars and their outstanding performance. By 1939 our sales of Jaguar cars were equal to all the distributorships which I had given up.

'After the war we took up the distributorship again with enhanced enthusiasm and I ran the old 3½-litre special at Shelsley Walsh in 1946 and 1947 still maintaining its position as one of the fastest cars regularly competing, until an unfortunate misjudgement on my part caused a crash which finished racing and speed events for me.

'Subsequently, as everybody knows, Jaguars went in for racing seriously and swept the board in sports car racing, and in doing so achieved success in this field which has probably never been equalled. There is no doubt that their enormous success at Le Mans and elsewhere did much to enhance their reputation abroad and to provide the data from which the outstanding qualities of present day Jaguars owe a tremendous debt.

'I suppose the biggest milestone in the Jaguar history was the introduction of the famous XK120 and the Mark VII with a similar engine. Since then Jaguar sales have increased nearly every year and the various new models introduced since that date have caused me to think back many times on my good fortune in having made a decision to concentrate on Jaguars to the exclusion of other distributorships.'

S.H. NEWSOME

From what I conjecture to be a Company press release

JAGUAR CARS AT MONZA   JULY 2nd, 1957

'A race on the banked circuit at Monza was held on Saturday June 29th. The race was 500 miles divided into three heats and is probably the fastest race ever held in Europe.

'Nine American racing cars had been brought over from the U.S.A. These cars had all been specially built for the Indianapolis 500 miles race, the premier race in America.

'Originally it was arranged for these cars to race against the European Racing Stables, but eventually all European cars were withdrawn.

'At very short notice by special request from the organisers Jaguar Cars agreed to compete with their three D-type Jaguars to give a European challenge to the race. Two of the D-type Jaguars which were competing in the race were the two winning cars from the Le Mans 24 hour race. Owing to the difficulty of transport and the short time between the two events, these cars had to be run in the exact condition in which they finished Le Mans. Further, owing to the limited time, the cars had to use normal section racing tyres as compared with the larger section track racing tyres which were being used by the American cars. For this reason the cars had to be limited to a maximum speed of 150 miles on the banked circuit, a speed well below the maximum of which the D-type is capable.

'Order of finishing showed three American cars in the first three places with the three Ecurie Ecosse D-type Jaguars placed fourth, fifth and sixth. The other six American cars which were competing failed to complete the full course.

'The achievement of the Jaguar D-type sports car constitutes a remarkable feat of endurance, particularly when it is recalled that two of the cars had already completed the 24 hours Le Mans course at a record speed.

'The speed of 148 mph that Jaguar achieved in this race represents the highest speed at which any sports car in the world has ever completed a race.

'The American cars which were competing were all single-seater cars run on special fuel. These cars had been specially built with the chassis offset to reduce the weight on the outer wheels and as these special cars are only capable of running one way on the circuit the race was run the opposite to the normal direction. This again put additional handicap on the Jaguar, which was a normal two-seater sports car with R.H. drive and furthermore running on normal pump fuel.

'The Dunlop road racing tyres of exactly the same type as used on the 24 hours race performed faultlessly on all three cars, despite the high loading caused by this exceptional track and the extremely high temperature of the day.'

Fred Gardner was one of the legendary 'characters' of Jaguar. Superintendent of the Wood Mill, he physically terrified anyone who came near the place and was absolutely unique in being the only employee that Lyons ever addressed by his first name! (Jaguar Cars)

Min. Fenton

JAGUAR COVENTRY CR 1G184 BOLOGNA 10 24   1250 =
JAGUAR COVENTRY TELEX =
BEST CONGRATULATIONS YOUR MAGNIFICENT PERFORMANCE LEMANS =
WEBER
++
JAGUAR COVENTRY

24 JUN 1957

After Ecurie Ecosse had won Le Mans for Jaguar in 1957, Weber Carburettors sent this telegram to the British firm.

Amongst a number of organisations which did an excellent job for Jaguar by producing a most successful sports racing car into which the XK engine was mounted, was the Cambridge engineering firm of Lister.

GEORGE LISTER AND SONS, LIMITED

Machinists and Engineering Craftsmen since 1890

Abbey Road, Cambridge - 'Phone: 55601/2/3 Wires: Welding, Cambridge

REGD. TRADE MARK

Our ref: BHL/TBR/MM

Your ref:

BRIAN LISTER (LIGHT ENGINEERING) LIMITED

Manufacturers of Engineering Components and The Lister Sports/Racing Car Chassis

Abbey Road, Cambridge - 'Phone: 55602

18th November, 1957.
BHL/TBR/JM.

Mr. Heynes,
Messrs Jaguar Cars Ltd.,
Coventry.

In actual fact, and it seems remarkable today, the D-types did not sell like hot cakes, and subsequent owners had some difficulty in divesting themselves of examples. Jaguar themselves ended up with a surplus hence the move, in late 1956, to produce the XKSS.

The ideal registration on Campbell McLaren's XKSS. (Philip Porter)

Tommy Sopwith in his Mark I saloon enjoyed many an entertaining dice with Mike Hawthorn similarly mounted. (Jaguar Cars)

Alice Fenton admires Lyons's latest creation. I imagine the marquee to be seen in the background was probably erected for the launch. (Jaguar Cars)

When Jaguar bought Daimler, they inherited the SP250 model and had thoughts of replacing it with a successor before finally killing it off. (Jaguar Cars)

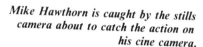

Mike Hawthorn is caught by the stills camera about to catch the action on his cine camera.

By my calculations there are 26 tubes in this D-type chassis. The way things seem to be going at present, should that chassis be discovered in a shed today it would enable 26 'genuine' cars to be built bearing that chassis number! (Jaguar Cars)

BILL RANKIN

'In the course of 27 years as PRO with this company, I have had to put out (often under protest) stories that were, shall we say, slightly exaggerated to such an extent that they were little less than downright inventions.'

A keen sporting Jaguar exponent in the Midlands was George Ward, a leading member of the Midland Automobile Club in the fifties and sixties. He used a succession of the small Jaguar saloons in hill climbs, such as the M.A.C.'s Shelsley Walsh sprints and rallies. (Mr. Ward Jnr)

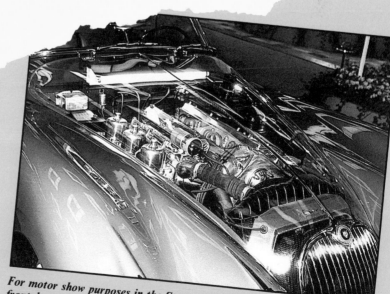

For motor show purposes in the States, Jaguar produced this full frontal see-through bonnet for an XK150. (Jaguar Cars US)

Les Bottrill seen in later years outside his US-based company.(Philip Porter)

<u>21st September, 1951.</u>

W. M. Heynes, Esq.,
Hotel Book-Cadillac,
<u>DETROIT. MICHIGAN. U.S.A.</u>

Dear Heynes,

          I do not know whether you have yet
seen the Salisbury axle people.

          If you have, you may already be
aware of the trouble we ran into with the T.T.
cars with the lower axle ratio, 3.54.   Three of
these failed on test at Lindley after approximately
150-180 miles, the trouble apparently being caused
by a breakdown in the film strength of the
lubricant. As a result of this, a higher viscosity
oil, S.A.E. 140 was tried.

          Bradley had been called in immediately
the trouble was experienced, but he was unable to
be helpful in any way.   We were using recommended
oil, G.X.90., which the oil people said should be
satisfactory.

          We then ran a fourth axle with the
S.A.E. 140 oil, which stayed put, but we had only
time to do 110 miles at Lindley.

          Unfortunately, this was on the Friday
before the cars had to leave on the Monday and,
although I was very disturbed at the idea of running
on the higher axle ratio, it appeared to be the only
safe thing to do, as the short test was not
conclusive that we should not have trouble in the race.

          However, England took two of the lower

          - contd. -

Whilst Heynes was over in the States on business in September 1951, he received this letter from his Managing Director. It is interesting to learn, amongst other things, that the prime motivation for adopting the Borg-Warner automatic transmission was a matter of supply rather than simply the desire to offer this type of transmission.

axle centres, which I told him to risk if
we were hopelessly over-geared.   Fortunately,
although the drivers did complain of being over-
geared, the cars seemed to be fast enough to win
as, of course, they proved to be.

          Bradley, incidentally, was most helpful.
He spent a good deal of time at the works, and at
Lindley, but freely admitted that he could not
understand the cause of the failure, and he is now
awaiting a report from America.

          I think the above brief details are
sufficient for you to follow up on the investigation
which is no doubt being made over there.

          We are in trouble with the cam shaft.
We have been receiving a tremendous number of
complaints regarding noise. As you know, I have
predicted this for a long time.   It has been found
that a satisfactory silent engine can be produced
by fitting E.N.V. camshaft, and it has now been
established (why it could not have been done before
I do not yet know) that the E.N.V. cam form is
not to drawing, whereas our own is, yet on the
evidence we have at the moment, we cannot obtain
the same silence on our own camshaft.   However,
since carrying out tests with different clearances,
it seems that we may be faced with having to obtain
new master cams for our Landis machine. Will you
enquire whether, if we have to do this, there is
any possibility of the job being done quickly.

I enclose drawings showing the difference between the E.N.V. and our own camshaft, from which you will see that there is a considerable variation.

- contd., -

Regarding the Borg-Warner box, it is imperative that we press ahead with this as soon as we can, as gearboxes are going to be a limiting factor in our production. I have done the best I can with Moss Gears, but they will not promise us more than 85 a week. They have, in fact, been giving us 65 only, and it is more than likely that they will not keep their new promise.

Will you let me know what delivery Borg-Warner can give. I think we should endeavour to schedule 50% of our production with this unit.

Incidentally, I have had a letter from Hornburg complaining that someone has returned to his part of California and is broadcasting that we are changing over to the Borg Warner box in the near future. Hornburg says this will have a very bad effect on his sales. It is essential that this matter, therefore, is treated in the utmost confidence.

I sent you a cable, as I found that Rankin had not done so, giving you the result of the T.T., although I presume you would already have some information about it. As we thought, Johnson was well down on the others, and actually fell to eighth or ninth position. He came in and handed over to Rolt, who, as I advised you in my cable, went like a bomb, but could not do better than pull up to fourth position. Two or three laps more, and he could easily have been third.

Yours sincerely,

(Drawings under separate cover. Air Mail.)

JOHN COOMBS, on his racing saloons

'The saloon started basically as a shell, two new shells in fact, without the underseal. The underseal was 35/40 pounds weight of gunge, plus the lead used on the joints. The interior of the doors was taken out, so we didn't have any winders, apart from the driver's door. It didn't have a dashboard, of course. That was the one thing that the homologation didn't specify that it had to have. So we didn't have any dashboard or fillets, or anything like that, and no headlining.

'The car got down to 24 cwt, which was an illegal weight. So we had to lead-weight the car. We used sheet lead on the floor at the back and the front. It was quite an interesting exercise trying to balance the cars. In the end if you took it out, it didn't make any difference – you could never make any difference!

'I remember doing a test day with Graham, with Roland's toolbox, which was a double handle job that would take two men to lift. We put it in the boot and the car still did the same speed around Goodwood. It was no different. It didn't create more understeer, or more oversteer, which was an amazing thing.

'I think the legal weight was 26 cwt, so therefore we had to ballast them up, but we got the weight down from the top to the bottom where we wanted it.

'We got down to two-leaf springs, which we had to hide for a long time! I don't know whether that one was ever caught up with!

'We used to cover the suggested five or six springs at the back with tape, and hope nobody ever broke the tape to see what was inside. In actual fact, it was pieces of plywood.

'They worked very well with two leaves on the back. We did away with the rubber between the springs because this created a problem for us as the axle used to tramp, and could move back and forward in the rubber. So we did away with all rubber. Eventually, we employed the stainless steel wire used in yachts to hold the mast, and we got up to something unbelievably high, such as five tons breaking strain on the cables that went from the rear axle to the suspension point on the body. We managed, on the first test session, to break those off, so we had to strengthen it up, and eventually we used those throughout. That, at last, stopped the axle tramping, which had been terrible. There was an unbelievable vibration period, which we managed to stop by doing that.

'Plus, we bent the rear axle. We got toe-in on it, which I thought up till then was impossible. Many times I would agree with you that it would be impossible.

'However, we bent the main axle casing, and then forced the drive shafts into the diff, and three-quarters of an hour driving around Goodwood, and we had worn them in. That was the method of getting toe-in on the back axle, which worked.

'We gained fractions of a second on all these things we did. It was quite satisfying.'

———————

'We were invited by Harry Weslake to give him an engine and he would improve on the performance of it. This we did. We gave him an engine over-bored to the maximum allowed and with a raised compression ratio, and sent it up to Harry Weslake.

'We were without the engine for a few weeks, and eventually we got a call saying. "Jolly good news – engine ready for you – 264 bhp," which really was magic.

'So we rushed a mechanic to Rye, he returned with the engine, we fitted it and called up Graham. Took both cars to Goodwood, whereupon it was slower – considerably slower.

'At that time the 3.8 engines were giving 222 bhp, that was the best we ever saw. So our 222 was quicker than the 264 bhp. So I got hold of Mr Weslake and told him our problem, whereupon he said, "Nonsense. You must have fitted the engine incorrectly".

'We replied that it was a pretty simple thing to do: "You just drop it in and pipe it up".

"Nonsense. Bring it to Brands Hatch." Arrived at Brands Hatch with Graham at the wheel and rapidly proved that the Mark II number one car was faster than the Mark II number two car. Engine was removed, taken to Rye, telephone rang later, "found where the problem is. It was carburettors. Drop it back in again. You'll find it will be fantastic."

'The engine never did work, It never ever worked. So we advertised one 264 bhp engine, got a very good price for it, and that was the end of that!

'He had this great dislike of Sopwith, that's why he called me. He wanted to see every race won by a Coombs car, rather than a Sopwith one, and we were very pleased to help him with that problem! He was very kind, he virtually did it for nothing too – but it didn't bloody well work!'

———————

I asked John Coombs how his racing relationship with Jaguar Cars started.

'I met Lofty. I suppose Lofty being Service, and I'm always moaning about the product, that's why I met him. Plus he was interested in motor sport, at the same time as myself.

'The first car he modified for me was a 3.4 Mark I that Ron Flockhart drove. He also let me have a Mark I 2.4, which I drove. It blew the water hose off the heater on the second lap and filled the interior of the car with steam!

'I came into the pits and I wasn't aware that you had to use the tools provided by the manufacturer in the car to do the running repairs. So you can imagine, I arrived in the pits, lifted the bonnet, found the hose off, and screamed for screwdrivers and what I needed.

'England shouted back at me, "Bloody fool, you've got to use the toolkit in the car".

'In those days, I didn't even know where it was kept!

'I always had a very good relationship with Lofty. Strained on many occasions but still a superb relationship with a wonderful guy.'

JOHN COOMBS

Letter from Birfield Limited, 1 March 1957:

Dear Mr. Heynes,

I was much saddened to hear from Mr. Power, that you felt resentful of the way in which Hardy Spicer had recently increased prices. I am quite certain that, if you knew the circumstances in which these prices had been reached, you would realise how, for years past, we have been absorbing a large percentage of the increased costs of manufacture, without passing them on to our customers. It was only possible for us prior to June 1956, to supply you without loss because of the exceptionally large volume of production during the car boom. Even then, the profit we made on sales to you and other car manufacturers was fractional.

Since then, we have supplied the passenger car companies at a loss – a loss that we carried for a short time by the back-log of spares supplies. This back-log has now disappeared. We did not increase our prices until it was clear that the over-all profit margin was dwindling dangerously.

In the last two years we have taken necessary steps to improve our research and development facilities, and we are making every endeavour to improve the quality of our product. Experience has shown that we must also be prepared, at short notice, to raise finance to keep abreast of your increasing demands – and we have great faith in the continuing increase in Jaguar cars in particular. We can do neither of these things if we are supplying you and the other car companies at a loss.

It is thus sad that, because the car trade has been over-indulged by us in the past, we now appear to some of our customers to be inconsiderate in advancing our prices.

Please do not think for one moment that I resent your feeling. I understand it. I also understand that we must never embark on a programme of absorbing expenses in future, when most of the people in the component industry are advancing their prices with each increase in cost and thus maintaining their profit margins.

I am sure you will be interested to know that the comparable prices at which your European competitors are buying propeller shafts is anything from 30% to 100% higher than the price at which we supply you.

We hold Jaguar Cars in the highest possible esteem, and you and your collegues equally so. I do hope you will realise that any strictures which you pass upon us cause us great disappointment. At the same time, we realise that perhaps our unobtrusive generosity in keeping prices down in the past has, unhappily, made us the target for what we feel is unreasonable, but quite understandable, criticism.

I was hoping to see you on Thursday next, when Sir William Lyons had kindly invited me to luncheon. In view of the disastrous fire you suffered, I am writing to ask if he would prefer that I postpone my visit to a later date – disappointed as I should be if this is necessary.

I do hope that you are successfully overtaking the immense difficulties you must all have been caused by this dreadful misfortune, and that you will soon be in full production again.

Yours sincerely,
H.E. HILL

Jaguar were unimpressed and five days later Arthur Whittaker, who had a widespread reputation for very tough, though fair, bargaining, sent an internal memo to Sir William Lyons on the subject.

After showing a breakdown of Hardy Spicer costs and estimated costs at which Jaguar's own machine shop could produce three types of prop shaft, the in-house costs were marginally keener in each case. It was only a matter of shillings, but it was by watching even such small amounts that Jaguar made such cheap cars and offered their famous value for money.

Whittaker, whom Heynes insists played a vital role in the Jaguar story, concluded his memo with the following.

'During the past few years we have met basic labour and material increases, which have been proportionate to those applied by other major suppliers. Accordingly their prices, prior to any increase, are only reasonable compared with other major component figures. Whilst they were quite helpful on prices in the early post war period, once we changed specifications on the introduction of the Mark VII and XK models, necessitating double shafts, it was always considered by us that earlier possible benefits were lost as a result, for the new figures were never regarded as being as favourable. This matter was discussed with them on a number of occasions without our being able to persuade them into our way of thinking.'

SIXTIES

Letter from W. Ronald Flockhart, BSc, AMI, Mech E. (Ron Flockhart – Ecurie Ecosse driver and winner of Le Mans in 1956 and 1957)

7th April, 1961

Thank you for your letter of 31st March, – I apologise for the delay in replying but I have only just returned from honeymoon.

One impression I have of the D-type Jaguar which is probably unique, is that its handling characteristics are similar to that of the "D" type ERA.

I found at Le Mans, particularly with the tail fin, that the faster it went the more stable the car became. It was my practice to relax completely down the Mulsanne Straight (race traffic permitting!) and flex my fingers and arms, the car steering itself at around 170 mph. A good personal test of the Chicken or Hero Driver was to take the slight right hand kink at the end of the Mulsanne Straight absolutely flat – an honest 5,800 rpm on the 1957 3.8 litre. It could be done, but only just. If the track was damp, then this game was for Chicken Drivers only. Both Ivor and I discovered this in our own fashion – something the spectators missed! However, in conditions of crosswind, this was not possible and I recall once at Goodwood one blustery day at practice where the Jaguar tail fin was a handful through Fordwater and past the pits.

The 3.4-litre Jaguar engine (and the later 3.8 litre) in my opinion come under the same category as the Gipsy Major and Rolls-Royce Merlin aero engines – it feels as if it would go on for ever. However the 3 litre version was never as successful. I don't think the design lent itself to continued operation above 6,000 rpm.

There was no marked difference in performance between the Lucas fuel injection 3.8 litre Jaguar and the normal Weber carburettor D-type. The only noticeable difference was that the Lucas injection gave smoother acceleration with no spitting back and hesitation round a slow corner on part throttle.

I still consider the 3.8 litre Jaguar engine to be capable of winning Le Mans at a higher speed than our 113 mph of 1957, if mounted in a suitable chassis – the E-type perhaps?

RON FLOCKHART

The 26th Annual General Meeting of the company was held on Thursday, 31 March 1960

The Chairman, Sir William Lyons, stated: 'Before opening the meeting, I would like to refer to the sad loss which our company has sustained by the untimely death of our Director of Home Sales, Miss Fenton. For over 35 years Miss Fenton served me, personally, and our company, with such single-minded loyalty and devotion to duty that I find it difficult to pay tribute to her in adequate terms.

I feel sure you will wish to join me in offering sincere condolences to her relatives, and will agree that our deep regret at the loss of a loyal colleague be recorded in these proceedings.'

Following the meeting Mr S. Glover proposed a vote of thanks with these words: 'On behalf of the shareholders, I take this opportunity of congratulating you, Mr Chairman, your fellow Directors, Executive Directors and Staff for the inspiring manner in which you have so ably and successfully conducted the affairs of this company, and I convey to you our sincere wishes for the future.'

The full meeting signified their unanimous approval of Mr Glover's remarks.

DAVID MURRAY of ECURIE ECOSSE; extracts from comments made in correspondence

THE RELATIONSHIP
'There has never been any official liason between Ecurie Ecosse and Jaguar Cars Limited. Ecurie Ecosse has simply been a customer who has been given the first opportunity of purchasing the previous year's competition cars from the factory.'

TECHNICAL CO-OPERATION
'In cases, Ecurie Ecosse has been able to point out to Jaguars certain suggested improvements but on the other hand Jaguar developments and improvements passed on to the Ecurie Ecosse greatly out-number the former.'

ON THE 1957 MONZANOPOLIS
'The Monza cars ran virtually standard in 1957. A dash from Le Mans to Monza was followed by a quick decoke and the transferring of scoops which were used at Le Mans to cool the brakes, to act on the tyres.'

ON THE 1958 MONZANOPOLIS LISTER
'The Ecurie Ecosse Lister Jaguar Monza single-seater was converted after the Monza race into a two-seater

sports which was eventually crashed, as many of the other EE Jaguars were, by Masten Gregory!'

ON THE 3-LITRE ENGINE BUILT FROM A 2.4-LITRE UNIT:
'The bored and stroked 2.4 model was the idea of Ecurie Ecosse (not necessarily the idea of W.E. Wilkinson!) and was carried out by Wilkie.'

ON POWER OUTPUTS
'The highest brake horsepower which was obtained from a Jaguar was from a 3.8 engine. This was 314 bhp but one must remember this engine was tuned for reliability and not for maximum speed. It is certain that more horsepower could be obtained from this engine if it was tuned for short periods and not for the longer distance races Ecurie Ecosse has been competing in.

'Regarding the 2.4 engine which was modified to 3 litres, a horsepower in excess of 265 was obtained but again this engine was prepared for 24 hours of Le Mans. This particular engine was lying second after $13^{1}/_{2}$ hours during the 1960 race when the car retired with a mechanical fault.'

ON MAXIMUM SPEEDS:
'I believe the maximum speed obtained from any D-type was 192 mph. This was achieved by the late-Mike Hawthorn in the 1956 Le Mans race. The car was a fuel injection model with a small wrap-round windscreen. After

Young William Lyons had worked for Brown & Mallalieu in Blackpool and later appointed them to be agents for his Swallow cars.

the 1956 race, the regulations were altered and larger screens had to be fitted. This brought the speeds down and our maximum speed on the Mulsanne Straight was 180 mph in 1957. In later years, the engine capacity was reduced and the highest speed officially recorded on the Mulsanne Straight, from a 3-litre Jaguar engine, was 160 mph. This was recorded by an Ecurie Ecosse car and is officially faster [see below] than the time set up by the 3-litre prototype E-type Jaguar which was entered for the 1960 race.

'The 1958 Lister-Ecurie Ecosse-Jaguar single-seater car which was used at Monza was, in fact, no faster than the D-types, due to the fact that the front wheels used in this race were out of proportion to the size of the car and were, therefore, a handicap. A slightly smaller wheel would have produced much greater speeds, mainly owing to reduced frontal area.'

DAVID MURRAY

N.B. According to the factory paperwork on the 1960 Le Mans race, the prototype E-type, E2A, achieved a speed of 167 mph.

On 24 October 1960, a year after the 3.8-litre engined version of the Mark II had been introduced, a Project Specification was issued by Claude Baily, together with instructions to proceed, to the Competition and Production Departments. The internal order number ZX548/02/2 was for 'One 3.8-litre Mark II Grand Tourismo Project car. R.H. Drive'.

'An unpainted bodyshell was modified by the Competition Department. All the following points to be checked for effective welding, and augmented where necessary with extra welding

and stiffeners. Front body cross-member welded along top and bottom edges, longitudinal members edge welded inside and outside over whole length of engine compartment, diagonal brace to valances and rear cross-member to seat pan welded every two inches. Torque arm brackets on seat pan, rear upper damper fixings, and rear road spring channels fully welded.'

Additionally, the nearside valance was to be modified for air duct trunking from the radiator, and that on the offside was to be altered to give

clearance for the three SU carburettors. Alterations were to be made to the boot to accept the battery and an auxiliary petrol tank. Additional kick-up channels were to be welded into the rear wheel arch area to form a box section with adequate clearance to handbrake cables. A stiffening plate was to be added to the dash structure and provision made for a horizontal clutch master cylinder. Not surprisingly after the problems experienced with the Panhard rod mounting, a new design of bracket and pin were to be welded in place.

Special fitments included a laminated screen and competition bucket seats trimmed in leather.

Inspiration for this concept may possibly have been provided by the Coombs modified cars, though apart from their own competition cars, only one Mark I was modified and the first Mark II did not receive the "Coombs treatment" until 1960.

Whatever the inspiration, a single car was commenced though the project, obviously, faded away.

The Daimler company was purchased on the 4 July 1960 for £3,110,000 and 'the excess of current assets over current liabilities'.

D-type Jaguar in immaculate condition, finished in pale blue, fitted 3.4 engine. Powr-Lok diff., R5 tyres, total mileage 6000, first registered May 1960, any trial, £1550 ono. Exchange considered. HP can be arranged.
November 1960

C-type Jaguar. D specification. Fitted 45 DCOE Weber carbs. Dark blue. good tyres. Chassis No. 021 Immaculate condition. Full width perspex screen, also touring screen and hood, full tonneau. Taxed to March 1963. £575.

C-type Jaguar. Very good condition. History known, never bumped or damaged. Sell or exch. vehicle with more weather protection.
August 1962

Extract from 'LIST OF INFLUENTIAL OWNERS OF JAGUAR CARS' 1960/61

H.M. Queen Elizabeth, Queen Mother	Jaguar Mark VII
H.M. Queen Marie of Yugoslavia	Jaguar Mark VIII
H.R.H. Prince Georg of Denmark	Jaguar 2.4 Litre
Viscountess Plumer	Jaguar 2.4 Litre
The Lord Ogilvy	Jaguar Mark VII
The Marquis of Cholmondley	Jaguar XK140
Lord Allerton	Jaguar XK140
Lord Kimberley	Jaguar XK150
Sir George Young	Jaguar Mark VII
H.E. The Argentine Ambassador	Jaguar Mark VIII
H.E. The Iranian Ambassador	Jaguar Mark VIII
Cornelia, Countess of Craven	Jaguar Mark VIII
Lady Seabright	Jaguar XK120
The Marchioness of Bute	Jaguar 2.4 Litre & open XK
Lady Hulton	Jaguar XK150
The Nawab of Bhopal	Jaguar XK140
H.E. The Mexican Ambassador	Jaguar Mark VIII
Robert Morley	Jaguar Mark VIII & 3.4 Litre
Louise Rainer	Jaguar Mark VII
Lloyd B. Nolan	Jaguar Mark VII
Alfred Marks	Jaguar 2.4 & 3.4 Litre
David Nixon	Jaguar Mark VIII
Norman Wisdom	Jaguar 3.4 Litre
Ronald Colman	Jaguar Mark VIII
Yvonne de Carlo	Jaguar Mark VII
Anita Eckberg	Jaguar XK140
Count Ladislas de Hoyos	Jaguar 2.4 Litre
Air Commodore Douglas Iron	Jaguar 2.4 Litre
Marquis of Bristol	Jaguar XK? F.H.C.
Count Munster	Jaguar 3.8 Litre
Spencer Tracy	Jaguar XK? D.H.C.
Stan Freburg	Jaguar 3.4 Litre
Uruguayan Ambassador to Holland	Jaguar 2.4 Litre
Pakistani Ambassador to Holland	Jaguar Mark IX
Chilean Ambassador to Holland	Jaguar Mark IX
Rt. Hon. The Earl of Bradford	Jaguar 3.8 Litre
Sir Robert Ropner	Jaguar 3.8 Litre
S.A.S. Prince Rainier of Monaco	Jaguar 3.8 Litre
Briggs S. Cunningham	Jaguar 3.8 Litre
Noel Cunningham-Reid	Jaguar 3.8 Litre
George Formby C.B.E.	Jaguar 3.8 Litre
The Duke of Kent	Jaguar 3.8 Litre
Count Pozzo di Borgo	Jaguar 3.4 Litre
Baron Malfatti	Jaguar 3.4 Litre
His Grace The Duke of Somerset	Jaguar 3.4 Litre
The Hon. Gerald Lascelles	Jaguar 3.8 Litre
The Earl of Jersey	Jaguar 2.4 Litre
The Earl of Strathmore	Jaguar Mark IX
The Hon. Marquess of Dufferin and Ava	Jaguar 3.8 Litre
Robert Glenton	Jaguar 3.8 Litre
The Rt. Hon. The Viscount Portman	Jaguar Mark IX
Lord Charles Spencer-Churchill	Jaguar 2.4 Litre
Sheikh Ghanim bin Ali Althoni	Jaguar 3.4 Litre
Rt. Rev. G.A. Beck, Bishop of Salford	Jaguar 3.4 Litre
Nano de Silva-Ramos	Jaguar 3.8 Litre
Graham Hill	Jaguar 3.8 Litre

None of these frontal treatments found their way onto a particular car, but elements of Mark II, Mark X and XJ6 are clearly recognisable.

Below: *A policeman's lot must have been quite a happy one, driving around in Mark IIs all the time. Indeed they were an ideal car for dashing up and down the newly-opened M1 Motorway. Note the CID car in the centre foreground! (Jaguar Cars)*

Test report on Daimler SP250 (chassis number 1066)

7th April, 1961

From: Mr. N. Dewis
To: Mr. Heynes

Copies to Sir William Lyons, Mr. England, Mr. Baily, Mr. Knight and Mr. Simpson.
At the request of Mr. Heynes a road test has now been completed on the above car.

ENGINE:
Tappet noise very audible.
Several rubber hoses on induction manifolds show signs of leaking.
Idling on occasions very lumpy and uneven.
Performance not impressive on low speed pick-up.
Heavy vibration from exhaust system.
CLUTCH:
Slips badly during full torque gear changes.
GEARBOX:
Gear lever chatters at high rpm.
1st. 2nd. and 3rd. gears very noisy.
AXLE:
Rejected for noise – pulling light load.
STEERING:
Very sticky on lock.
Heavy steering kick.
Knock from steering column.
Difficult to manipulate steering wheel lock nut.
RIDE AND HANDLING:
Ride has much to be desired, excessive pitching from rear end, becomes airborne over long wave pitching surface, also hits bump stops very forcefully.
Damper settings and spring rates could be improved.
One thing I suspect is misalignment of the front and rear track, the rear track would appear to be offset to the N/S the width of a tyre in relation to the front track.
Far too much wheelspin is evident when leaving slow corners with full power "on", a Powr-Lok diff would be an asset.
Insufficient roll at rear end.
BRAKES:
Pedal effort rather high for low speed check braking.
Rear brakes seem to lock early in an emergency stop, what is the back to front ratio?
Axle tramp noticeable when braking on rough surfaces.
Position of handbrake restricts seat adjustment.
COOLING:
Water temperature recording 95°C during six laps of the outer circuit at MIRA driving at 100+ mph, this seems to be rather high .
Is the air entry through the grille adequate?
STABILITY:
Car moves sideways very sharply in a cross wind, movement influenced by rear end.
PEDALS:
These are set too much to the O/S, impossible to heel and toe, one has to "feel" around for the accelerator.
BODYWORK:
Bonnet shake very noticeable on rough roads.
Depth of windscreen too narrow.
Door hinges very weak – vertical shake.
Door lights gape at top edge during high speed driving.
Better insulation of the scuttle and refitting of several grommets would reduce engine noise.

---

100 Jaguar shares bought in 1952 at 24/- (£1.20) would, by 1961, give 900 shares at 78/9 (£3.94).

Codenames

Utah – Pressed Steel Fisher codename for Mark II/S-type/420 bodies
Zenith – codename for Mark X saloon

XK120 Drophead, 1951, finished in Carmen Red, seat covers, wood rim steering wheel, new tyres, perfect mechanical order, £245.
£165!! 1951 XK120. Sound motor, off-white, red leather. Terms, etc.
November 1962

1938 2½-litre SS Jaguar. We believe this vehicle, due to its incredible condition and history, to be absolutely irreplaceable. Built in 1938 it was unused during the war years until 1948, since then it has covered 58,000 miles with a new high compression engine fitted 6000 miles ago (bills available). The vehicle can only be described as looking and running like a new motor car and represents unrepeatable value to the enthusiast at £225.
May 1963

Seats very poor in respect of comfort and back support, back rest twists with body movement when cornering.
Ends of tubes unsightly and roughly finished with seat backs folded down.
Rear fasteners for securing detachable hard top appear unsightly.
Bonnet safety catch difficult to release.
Demisters not very effective on windscreen.

GEORGE MASON, Superintendent of the Experimental Department and former Superintendent of the Competition Shop.

On development of the Daimler 2¹/2-litre saloon and fitting of the Daimler V8 engine in the Jaguar small saloon shell.

'We started with a Mark I because in those days they wouldn't give us a Mark II body to put it in!

'We had a Mark I that used to be the Dunlop air suspension car. The car was absolutely rotten. Lofty had been talked into the idea and he was all for it. We went ahead and used that body which stood outside the mill, with all flat tyres and everything. It was practically welded to the ground, it had been there that long!

'We got it in and stripped it out. We welded up all the spare holes in the body, because it had been cut into to fit the Dunlop suspension and everything. We acquired a 2¹/2-litre engine and popped it in. To everybody's surprise – I'll never forget it – you could walk between the fan on the engine and the radiator. It looked so small and unloved in there!

'But we went on to develop it and, quite seriously, I think it was one of the best cars Jaguar ever put together.

'It would out-perform the 2.4. It would perform as well as the 3.4 and was certainly better on fuel economy. I would think, still today, it was the quietest car we'd ever made because, if you didn't look at the rev. counter, you wouldn't know the damn car was running.

'The car amazed everybody who drove it. We went a little bit over the top perhaps with the exhaust system. If I remember rightly, I put four silencers in each bank on that car. Quite seriously, you couldn't hear the damn thing running!

'When the model was released at the Motor Show in London, they'd got a car down there as a demonstrator, but it still wasn't as good as the old one we'd got here. So we took the engine out of the old one and it went in that demonstrator vehicle. We hadn't done anything special to the engine but it was a sweet one.

'That model, when it was released, was way over the book price, even when two years old. They just couldn't get enough of those cars – it really went down well.'

'Mr Heynes, to his credit used to go round this company every Friday. As to the Competition Shop, there were some days he used to damn well live in there. He was a different type of engineer to what you get today. He certainly wasn't remote. There was certainly no class distinction in that man.

'If you had got a good idea, he would let you go on and do it. I've got nothing but admiration for the man – he was a gentleman of the first order.

'He'd get a bit tetchy when you didn't agree with him, but that was his right, obviously.

'He used to be in our shop an awful lot, to the point we used to get labelled as his "playpen", by a certain other top man.'

It was stated in May 1962 that 'the weekly wage bill of the Company in 1924 was £4. Today it is £150,000. 360 inspectors of quality and precision are employed, a ratio of one inspector to 10 production operatives.'

Even though the process was semi-mechanised, the lowering of the massive Mark X body onto its engine and suspension units, still seemed to need at least six pairs of hands. (Jaguar Cars)

This model, created by Malcolm Sayer, shows his first thoughts on the E-type shape. Note the two frontal treatments with the faired headlamp nearer the camera and a more traditional treatment on the other side. (Jaguar Cars)

TONY THOMPSON, OBE, British born former Head of Sales for Jaguar in the US, and later vice-president of the largest Rolls-Royce dealership in the world

'The guy who was in charge of advertising at the factory, Bill Rankin, was the man who absolutely knew how to project the right mixture of image. He thought up the idea of "Grace, Space and Pace". If he had been 50 years of age today, he would probably be the head of an advertising company in America.

'He was that sort of guy. A man who had a brilliant idea of the concept. By and large the Brits didn't use to talk about advertising a lot. Bill Rankin understood that what he had to do was project the Bentley Mark VI image.

'Lofty once said that it was Sir William's great delight to put a Jaguar Mark V beside a Bentley Mark VI – which is, of course, why we never made a Jaguar Mark VI, or indeed, why they never made a Bentley Mark VII – and walk down the street. He would then say to whoever he was walking with, "I am going to ask you to turn round and tell me of those two cars behind you, which one is the Jaguar".

'It was absolute plagiarism!'

'Lyons was amazingly autocratic. If he had something to say, he would say it. I had a couple or three funny experiences with him. He really found it very hard to tolerate any customer criticism. He did not like that.

'I would think it was at the '59 Motor Show in New York. I was on the stand as a young thing, 27 years old. Sir William came on the stand mit everybody – Jo Eerdmans and all the Vice-Presidents of the company, and when you're 27 a Vice-President seems very senior.

'There was a very difficult New Yorker, who I knew and who had been talking to me about all the things he hated about his XK140. Suddenly he turned round and said to me, "Tony that's him. That's Sir Lyons."

'I said, "Yes, that's Sir William".

'He stated he was going to talk to him and so he went over to Sir William, and I don't know what they said to start with but he came back to me with Sir William in tow. Sir William said to me, "Thompson, I want to see this man's car, which is in the garage". This was in the basement of the Coliseum which was where you parked in those days. They always had the Motor Shows there and they were held at Easter. Being Easter it was cold.

'So we went down to his car and the man said, "look, the heater doesn't work".

'Sir William said, "the heater does work".

'The car was started up, and the car had, if you remember, a Smiths heater with two little doors on it, and a control on the dash. I smoked and so he told me to light a cigarette. He held the cigarette – I'd no idea what he was going to do – he held it beside the heater and the smoke very gently wafted away.

' "Look," he said, "it works perfectly".

' "Sir Lyons, temperatures get to 15 below zero."

' "Young man," he said, "you just put on an overcoat" '.

JOHN MORGAN, who has held a number of senior posts concerned with overseas sales, including that of European sales director

'I joined Jaguar in '63 as Assistant Export Manager. I was then an Export Director for Europe for Rootes where I had been for 13 years. I speak languages, which helps, having had part of my education in Switzerland. So I feel pretty European.

'Sir William said he didn't offer people jobs, they had to apply for them!

'He'd been watching my progress and spoke to me one day.

' "I think you're the sort of person that would quite enjoy working with us, Morgan."

'I said, "Yes Sir William, I'd love to work for Jaguar".

' "Oh, you would, would you. Well, we don't offer jobs in this company. People have to apply for them. But if you'd like to apply, I think there is a good chance of you getting a job here."

'So I did, and I got it,' recalls John with much amusement. 'At £1400 a year!

'I took it on the condition made with Lofty that I would be, if satisfactory, made Export Manager within six months. The old boy who was the Export Manager was 76, and he'd been there since '49. All he did, frankly, was administer. He didn't like travelling. He wouldn't take a plane anywhere.

'He was a man called Ben Mason, a wonderful old chap, who was at Standard and then Singer. He was a splendid old boy who spoke about seven languages he'd learnt himself. I admired him very much and I worked with him for six months.

'Then a very strange thing happened. We had brought out a new car called the S-type, which was being launched at Paris. Mr Mason didn't appear to be going. Mr England rang down one day and said, "Mason, aren't you supposed to be in Paris? We are launching a new car there tomorrow – the dealer launch."

' "I know, Mr England, but I haven't been invited by the distributor, so I am not going."

' "You don't have to be invited by the distributor. You've a perfect right to go. It's your market. Now get on your bike and get a plane."

' "Well, I can't possibly go now because it's too late to get the Golden Arrow today," he said. "If I take it tomorrow morning, I won't be there till the do is over."

' "Mr Mason, this is 1963, not 1863." Silence. The next thing was a buzz to me.

' "Morgan? Dai, get on your bike, you're going over to Paris tonight." I did my job successfully and spoke French to all the dealers, which is what they wanted, and came back. Very shortly after that we had an American advisor come in from Studebaker, a friend of Sir William's and a great friend of Bertie Henly's. He went round trying to advise Sir William and one of the things he suggested was that he should get rid of the old boys – one from Daimler and one from Jaguar.

'I came in one day from a little trip and I was suddenly told, "You are taking over tomorrow. Mr Hilton's been retired from Daimler".

'We had only bought Daimler out relatively recently and they were all complete with their own desks. It was very funny – they all had wooden desks and all the Jaguar people had steel desks, so you could pick out who were your Daimler people and who were your Jaguar people!

'A few days later Mason was retired and I took over both. Then six months later we formed a company called Jaguar Export Sales Limited, which I was a Director of. It was the first time we had had an Export Director at Jaguar. I took over all the exports, except America, and Sir William held that to himself for a long time. Eventually I persuaded him that he really ought to let me have America too, which he did.

'There was no faith in this company that America was a solid market. Sir William hated the American market because he had had some very bad early experiences with some of the distributors. One sued him – a terrible man who sued so many people and got away with millions of dollars in cases over franchising. When he didn't do the job, he was sacked, and then he'd sue the manufacturer. He got us for quite a bit of money and Sir William got served with a writ one day in the Waldorf Astoria, which he didn't like at all!

'So he did eventually hand over America, but he said, "I'm not going to accept crazy marketing plans for America, because I don't believe in it. It's a volatile market". They quite definitely and positively restricted the American market in the sixties, because they didn't trust the market as a solid market.'

Metalastik Ltd.,

December 9th, 1963

Dear Mr. . . . .,

Following an illustration of our car in the Automobile Engineer we have a letter from Mercedes claiming Patent Rights on the use of the 'V' mounting for suspension unit.

I think the whole thing is pretty far fetched. I have written to them and acknowledged their letter and stated that we are investigating, but from a preliminary inspection, we do not think that infringement can be claimed.

As these mountings are of your manufacture and in fact they were designed in collaboration with your engineers, I feel that I should very much like to have your advice on this matter.

I have not yet submitted the problem to our own Patent Agents and as Metalastik and Jaguar will both be involved, I think we might make some joint approach.

I enclose a copy of the Patent Specification, together with a copy of their letter. You will notice that the Application date is December 4th, which is certainly not before the date which we started experimenting with you on this type of mounting on the Mark I 2.4. I won't say any more until you have had a chance to look at the Patent and see the letter.

Yours sincerely,
W.M. HEYNES

Jo Eerdmans and Sir William Lyons, who had an unusually close relationship, discuss the Mark X model, which Eerdmans today refers to as 'the lemon' (Jo Eerdmans)

Jaguar Le Mans D-type. Supplied by Jaguars direct to present owner, costing with modifications £4600. British Racing Green. Unmarked. Never raced or rallied. 21,600 miles. Fastidiously maintained. 150 – 180 mph dependent on axle ratios. Absolutely unique for road work. Any reasonable offer above £1900 or part exchange transaction considered.

May 1963

Swallow *Coachbuilding Company (1935) Limited*

S I D E C A R S   19-31 ALBION ROAD · GREET · BIRMINGHAM 11

TELEPHONE: VICTORIA 1987-8   ·   TELEGRAMS: SIDECARS, BIRMINGHAM

Directors: R. G. J. WATSON, *Chairman* · G. C. BENNETT, *Managing* · V. WATSON · N. M. STEPHENS

ROY SALVADORI

Roy Salvadori was famous for his versatility which was amply illustrated on one occasion when he won no less than four races in a day: in a saloon car, a sports car, a sports racing car, and a Grand Prix car. During our discussions I mentioned that it was a shame we rarely, if ever, see the top racing drivers of today in anything other than a Formula One car.

'It is sad. It does help having the leading drivers competing as well. I am not saying that we drove any quicker than the other boy, because maybe we had better machinery, but it would be very nice if you could see Senna and Piquet in ordinary saloons.'

I reminded Roy of the BMW M1s that were run at the Grand Prix meetings a few years back.

'Yes exactly, that was marvellous racing. I used to watch that and to me that was just as good as the Grand Prix. That was great stuff. There is so much money involved you can understand why nobody wants to have a driver hurt and they are more likely to get hurt in that sort of stuff than they are in the Grand Prix, because you feel so safe in a saloon.

'You do things that you wouldn't think of doing in an open-wheeled car. You just lean on each other, normally – you'd hardly do that with a Grand Prix car; that can turn nasty.'

'Did you,' I asked, 'literally lean on each other when driving the Jaguar saloons?'

'Oh yes, not arf! I think my greatest trophy was presented to me at a Jaguar Apprentices Dinner at the factory. The trophy was a small flat panel from the side of a Jaguar car, and it was painted in Coombs' grey. On the side there were patches of green from the Berry car, and patches of blue from the Endeavour car, and . . . .

'After the race, you'd reckon to have a few odd colours on the side! But you could do it, and it was fairly safe. If you went inside somebody, and lent on them it saved the understeer. Normally you'd be understeering off the road, but if you could nail somebody by getting inside, you just touched them and that would stop your understeer, and get you through. Otherwise, you'd be off the road – you'd be going too quick to go into the corner, so you lean on him a bit and push him over, and you're through!

'That's only if you think you're going to be quicker than the other car, otherwise he's going to be scrabbling over you, and do the same thing to you. But at least it gets you through, and if you are quick enough you can go on. But you couldn't do that in a formula car. You'd lock wheels, and there'd be a terrible nonsense.

'You didn't do it so much in the E-type. That was a great thing for

The Swallow sidecar business was eventually acquired by the established firm of Watsonian, but they kept the Swallow name alive.

The Jaguar Trim Shop
Although Jaguar boasted the largest trim shop in Europe, Sir William Lyons would never allow it to be visited by those on factory tours. He felt that a sight of the mundane nature of the construction of seats, and the modest materials used in the unseen areas, would harm the Jaguar image and essential mystique.

XK120 Fixed Head. 1954. C-type modifications, 2 inch carbs, Michelin X tyres, Boranni steering wheel, musical horns, wireless, heater. Finished in pearl grey. £275.

May 1963

Trevor Taylor wishes to dispose of his immaculate 1960 3.8 Jaguar Mk II. Radio, Koni shock absorbers, gas flowed head, special exhaust system. £800 ono.
Mark I saloon, 3.8 E-type competition engine, 300 bhp. Wide angle head, etc., special clutch, overdrive and Konis. Wide track wheels and R6s, plus chromium plated wheels and Xs. 0–100 in 18.1 secs. Mark II white interior. Reutter seats, high ratio steering, roll-bar, etc., absolutely perfect. Must sell. All mods under 5000 miles. £600 ono – G. Marshall.

January 1964

saloon cars. I can't remember driving like that in anything other than a saloon car. They are pretty strong, you know.

'Twice driving Jaguars I have been very lucky with seat belts. Once was at Oulton Park when I had a tyre blow on a saloon, going into Cascades, I believe it's called, shortly after the start. A tyre blew and instead of taking the left-hand corner I went straight over the bank and into the pond! I was upside down, and trapped under water.

'You'd never get ordinary seat belts off, but John Coombs had got some very special ones from an aircraft. All you had to do was touch it, and they would "explode". I must have done that – I can't get my seat belts undone in an ordinary car now, even when it's the right way up.

'So I must have touched this and I was floating about in the bottom of the car. I was under water for a couple of minutes, and my chest was exploding. I thought this is the end. I started taking in water, and when I say water, it was foul water – the bloody pond stank so much I can't tell you!

'I'd given up and I was only half conscious when the marshalls jumped in and dragged me out of the back of the car. They'd been looking in the front, and found me floating in the back!'

Salvadori had the misfortune to have a massive accident on someone else's oil at 170 mph on the Mulsanne Straight at Le Mans. The speed differential has often been criticised over the years and Roy retains vivid memories of the problem.

'Those bloody creepers – mostly French. If you saw a blue car you knew you were in trouble. That was the difference in racing standards in those days. If you saw a green car, you'd be fairly happy about it. But if you saw one of these little blue creepers that were on this Index of Performance – you'd wonder what they were going to do! They weren't experienced drivers and you used to go through agonies. You'd see them miles ahead and you knew they were going to take the fast car line. There was no way they could creep round the inside – no, they were going to do a big drift. They didn't, actually, drift those things because they didn't have enough steam, but they would just take the racing line.

'The red cars were normally very quickly driven because they were faster cars, so you didn't have a problem with them. In fact, they were faster than we were, than the cars I drove. They would only overtake you on the straight.

'With the cars we were driving, nobody would really overtake you in a corner. Especially driving Astons; if you're going to be overtaken in a corner on the Aston, you're going to be sacked. That's where you made up all your time. We wouldn't expect to be overtaken in corners. You just watched your mirrors on the straight and kept to one side. The reason you are behaving is because it makes it safer for yourself if you keep out of the damn way.

'What these little creepers didn't understand was that they were going to get a sharp nudge up the chuff, and they were going to be hurt themselves.

'In fact, I did collect one once going through the Dunlop Corner past the pits in the wet. There was one of the little blue cars in the middle of the road. I thought, "Oh no. He's not going to get over. No."

'So I tried the inside and the car started to break away, and I thought if I go on the outside I'm going to collect the hedge. So I just lined myself right up on him, braked as hard as I dared and hit him straight up the arse.

'He went straight over the hedge!

'There's this guy waving his fists for the next few laps, because it was the end of his car. Do you know, I forgot about it after a few laps, and I thought the car felt alright. When I handed over to Reg Parnell, he asked how the car was.

"Fine, Reg." I'd forgotten all about it, as you could do. It was getting dark and after about half an hour, old Reg came in and said,

"All the lights are out of focus. They're shining up in the trees".

'The mechanics had a look and there was a bang underneath, and of course it had bent the headlamps and they had to reset them. I never heard the end of that from Reg Parnell, believe you me!'

I asked Roy how the DB3S and D-type compared and why the Aston was so much quicker round bends.

'It had to be . . . because it never really had the power! I would have thought it was development. It's like any car, you can get to a certain standard and then you develop it. I think that the Aston was developed right to the very, very end. There was nothing left. I would say that with the Jaguar there was further development potential.

'Jaguar had this wonderful shape, but the brakes were much better on the Aston. It was really hard work racing against a "D", because you had to nail them. They would leave you on the straight and the advantage we had was just on braking and cornering. If you were close enough, you could always overtake a "D" going into a corner. But if you didn't do it on the right corner, you'd had it.

'For instance, at Aintree it was no good overtaking the "D" on the corner before the straight – or two corners before the straight – because on the straight he would just muscle past. So really you had to do it at the end of the pit area and nail them there, or the next corner. Then you'd work like mad on the infield, just to be able to scrape enough time to get to the straight, and you'd see the Jaguar come tearing up on the straight. As long as you were ahead at Melling you had a chance.

'If we had clear circuits, we were on a par with each other's times on British circuits, so it was very difficult. When we were on the short circuits, it really got the Aston drivers a bad name, because you had to do some tricks to get in front of the D-types. You had to shut the door. You had to get them on the loose stuff a bit, so they couldn't use their power.

'The favourite trick when you overtook a "D" was not to go through the corner flat out, but to go through the corner at their speed and edge them over onto the loose stuff! If you could get them on the loose stuff, that would give you half a second, and that was all you needed. If you just drift into them, and keep your car there, and just get them on the grass or the loose stuff, you'd get your half second, because they wouldn't be able to put their foot down. If you could get them off-balance, then you'd be in front. Then it was up to you.'

Did Roy, I enquired, have any particular memories of the other driver's and the way they drove.

'Duncan was always rough. You could be rough with Duncan. I think you had to adapt your driving to the drivers. Moss was very, very good and very fair, and so was Rolt. So you would drive one way against one driver, and you'd be tough with another driver, because you were the same sort of types.

'You had the drivers who were very correct. I don't suppose I was terribly correct, but you'd have to, sort of, return the compliment. You wouldn't do a thing to Stirling – not that you'd have the opportunity because you probably wouldn't be near him – but you had to be correct with Stirling because he was a very correct driver. So you drove accordingly – at least that's what I used to do.

'If I knew anybody would chop me, I'd have the greatest delight in giving them the treatment! You'd say, "He can do it to me, so let me get there first"!'

Of Peter Walker, 'Very good driver. Not really underrated because everybody rated him. He was a nervous driver, a bag of nerves, but on his right days and his right years, he was as quick as anybody. Very good driver. Very game. Nice to have in the team.'

On his XK120, 'I loved it. I'd had a very big accident and needed something easy to drive. I won a few races with it, but it used to roll. I went to see Lofty who was very kind. He took me to a race circuit where

1954 XK120 FHC, maroon, silver wire wheels, radio, heater, screenwashers, twin exhaust, special rear seats. £195. HP, part exhanges . . .

February 1964

they tested the cars and got Peter Walker to drive it. He thought it was OK and that was all I needed – someone to tell me it was OK. In those days Peter was a star and I was just starting.

'I felt very chuffed that Lofty had bothered, but he always did bother. My next memories are of driving for Ecurie Ecosse in the C-type. I think the worst position I ever had with the Ecosse car was a second. I was pretty hairy in those days, bouncing off hedges and all sorts!'

Sir William Lyons congratulates Graham Hill, that great character and driver of the winning E-type upon its début appearance – to say nothing of protagonist in numerous thrilling dices with Salvadori and Parkes and victories in Mark IIs. (Jaguar Cars)

Jo Eerdmans introduces the Prime Minister, Harold Macmillan, to the Mark X in New York in 1962. (Jo Eerdmans)

BILL CASSIDY – one of the backroom boys

After an apprenticeship at Armstrong Siddeley, he joined Jaguar in 1945 and worked as a Chargehand in the Experimental Department. Later he became Senior Foreman of the Experimental Machine Shop and was concerned with the building of the Le Mans cars and Motor Show cars, amongst many others.

'The Competition shop was mainly started because the competition side was interfering with the model side in the Experimental.

'We'd build six competition cars in six weeks for Le Mans – it was really night and day work.

'I remember Norman Dewis was once testing axles at MIRA. We were sending out axles from the shop with two different ratios, and of course they had knock-on wheels. I was walking up the shop one afternoon when we were doing these and putting the hubs on. We had fitters at MIRA who were changing the axles for testing. I didn't notice but this one axle was upside down on the trestle. The fitter said to me, "which is left-hand?"

'I said, "For Christ's sake, that's left and that's right"!

'When the axle got to MIRA the fitter said to Norman, "This hub's on the wrong side". With knock on wheels, if you have the hub on the wrong side, the wheel can come off of course.

'Norman said, "Oh, it'll be all right. We'll chance it."

'Well he did, and the wheel did come off, at 140 mph! There was a spring plate on the rear end of the C-type made of spring steel which was at least a quarter of an inch thick and about four inches deep. The car had dropped on to that. When he stopped, he'd lost two inches of it! And the wheel was found about a mile away down an air raid shelter!

'These things happen when you are working under pressure. There were times when we worked till three o'clock in the morning, then back in again at eight o'clock, and sometimes right through the night for two nights without any sleep.

'I've been there with Sir William – he was Mister then – at two in the morning on the Show cars. He's been there as well, and he'd say, "I'll see you at seven o'clock, Cassidy". That was it. You were there, you didn't argue about it.'

———————

'We had moved from Swallow Road up to Browns Lane in '52, and the Experimental Department was the last to move. We didn't have a Foreman then. I was working on a milling machine one day at 12 o'clock, and at ten past I was the Foreman – that was how they worked!

'I saw Lyons talking to this chap called Bill Robinson, who was the Body Shop Superintendent, and he was more-or-less looking after our department from the discipline side. He was no engineer as far as the mechanics, but a brilliant bloke on jigs and fixtures.

'They were talking together and eventually Lyons said, "All right Robinson, I'll leave that with you".

'He came to me and he said, "Do you think you could run this shop?"

'I replied that I'd effectively been doing it for some time. "Right," he said, "there's your office". That was it.

'Once you had got Lyons's confidence, then you couldn't do anything wrong. But until you did, he was a very hard task master.

'When we used to do a show car, particularly the cars for the stand, he'd want it down as low as we could get it – the sleek look. I've even done Show models without exhausts on! I just put two tail pipes on!

'In the early hours of one morning we put the car on a ramp and lifted it up to the height of the stand. We then pulled the car down and clamped the suspension down. He said, "Now that's it, but what about those exhausts?"

Although it seems that Lyons was generally a shy, retiring man, his taste in clothes, as well as motor cars, tended towards the flamboyant at times.

The purchase of Guy Motors in 1960 is a good example of how astute Lyons was. He purchased the company from the Receiver for £800,000, and acquired tax losses of £2¹/4m. In the first year of Jaguar ownership, Guy made a profit of £300,000.

new grace.. new space.. new pace

There was no questioning that the Mark X had 'space'. By British standards it was massive.

Comedian Norman Wisdom is seen (centre) examining the brand new Mark X which stole the 1962 London Motor Show.

'So I said, "Let's take them off and I can put two dummy tail pipes out the back".

"Brilliant idea. You go ahead and let me see it." That's how you got his confidence.

'We always used to get a yearly bonus because we weren't paid for any overtime, and I used to do very well on the yearly bonus. Then I had a heart attack in '67 and I was off work for 26 weeks. It happened over Easter and the day after the holiday, he was in the Shop and somebody told him.

'"Oh," he said, "why wasn't I told?"

'I was in hospital and the sister came and asked if I knew anybody named Lyons. I replied that he was my boss. Apparently he had been on the phone asking how I was, and every day his secretary rang up. After a while I went back, not to work, but just to have a wander round the factory, and I saw him. Now in those days you only got paid for the first six weeks you were off and then it was up to Lyons.

'He said to me, "Don't worry about hurrying back and don't worry about your salary". I got paid the whole time I was away. He even said to me, "Are you happy with your treatment? If you're not, I'll send you down to Harley Street".

'He had been known to send his Foremen to Switzerland when they've been ill, for a week's holiday.

Of course, a number of people used Mark Is and IIs for competitive activities, but very few can have hillclimbed an S-type, as did George Ward seen here at Shelsley. (Mr. Ward Jnr)

£165 secures two XK120s. One in good mechanical and body condition, one with scruffy body but in good mechanical order.

April 1964

1954 XK120, cream, special equipment model, fixed head coupe, wire wheels, Michelin X tyres, radio, luggage rack, twin exhausts, new batteries, original condition. Enthusiast's car. Three owners only. £245 or offer. Must be sold.

November 1964

XK140 Roadster, 1956, new gearbox. One owner last six years, around £155. XK120. Body damaged. Four new tyres. Mechanically perfect, 120 mph. £60 ono.

October 1965

'I did all sorts of things. For example, I had put the XK engine in the first limousine and, as Lyons would say, "made it a runner". Sir George Harriman came to the works to look at this new Daimler. I had to put the Mark X suspension under it, but of course it was heavier than the Mark X, and so we didn't have the right springs on it. The chrome was stuck on with plasticine – it was just a "look at" car.

'I took it round to the front offices for Sir George Harriman to look at it with Sir William, and Mr Heynes was there of course. Heynes said to me, "Is it a runner".

'I said, "Yes, but for Christ's sake, don't take it on the road".

' "Oh it'll be all right." So they took it on the road. And the bloody bonnet flew up, 'cause it was only tied down!'

In what I take to be the sixties, a series of photographs were taken at the Browns Lane and Radford factories to illustrate 'Women in Industry'. (Jaguar Cars)

'I knew Mike Hawthorn well. We had the car that he was killed in back in the Shop. It was nearly cut in half by the tree he hit. The tree hit the offside and it went right through, nearly to the prop-shaft. He'd got no chance.

———————

'It was the same when young John Lyons got killed. He'd missed the ferry on the way to Le Mans, and they didn't wait for him. They were supposed to wait in Calais, but they couldn't wait. He was trying to catch them, and of course driving on the right-hand side of the road, he pulled out to overtake and an American army lorry hit him.

'They just dumped the car in the Channel. It creased the Old Man. John had just joined the firm, and when Sir William brought him round to meet all the Foremen he said to me, "This is Mr John", but I knew him as John. He used first names with me because I'd known him when he was a small lad, when he used to come in the factory. It was the same with Jonathan Heynes. I remember him when he used to come to the factory with his dad at about three years of age. We had pedal cars in here for him before Christmas!

'I was in the Press and on television when we had the factory fire, because I rang for the brigade. We were working overtime and it was reported to me that they had seen smoke. So I picked up the phone and rang the gate, and told them to get the Brigade, and I told them to get the City Brigade as well, because it looked as if it was in the tyre stores.

'As it spread, we were pulling the finished cars out because it was travelling along the roof and the bitumen was dropping on to the cars, and they were catching fire. We got most of them out. Then the sawmill was next door, so we had to get rid of all the wood. We pulled tons of that out.

'Eventually the Brigades arrived, Birmingham, Coventry and Solihull Brigades were all there. That was a fire. It frightened you to death; when you see a wall 100 yards long, 20 foot high just glowing red . . . .

'Next day I was interviewed on BBC and ITV television as the person who'd given the alarm. I don't know who'd told them but they'd got it all wrong. They'd got me down as Chief Tester. I said to Norman Dewis: "You've lost your job"!

––––––––––

'I can tell you a story about the Mark V. We made the first chassis in the shop. It was about four inches wide and six inches deep, and they were using a block to hammer the metal over. Some bloody fool left the block in and welded the whole lot up!

'The block must have weighed 60 or 70 lbs. We had to cut the blooming thing open to get the block out!

'Another story I can tell you is about the D-types. We were building the cars for Le Mans and the body fitters came along with the top skins. There was the centre section, and these are riveted every $3/4$ inch. Where the top met the bottom half and the door line, they had to be argon arc welded.

'While this "U" section was open there were drawings in there and so many blokes around you couldn't see the car. They were round the back, under the car, putting the pedals in, and you were stepping on men to get in the car. These body blokes came with the top skin with the two cockpits cut out, laid it on, put a couple of pins in, marked it and took it away, and took some more off.

'I always remember Heynes came in the Shop and I was standing watching these men. They put the pins and marked it. "Bloody hell," he said, "they're not taking it off again. Rivet it up."

'So of course they got the rivets out and the old guns were going riveting this thing up. That was all done and they carried this body in to be welded up. Meanwhile one of my blokes kept saying he'd lost his hammer. Anyway the body was welded up and somebody happened to look down the hole for the steering column, and there was the ball end of a hammer!

'I daren't say don't weld because Heynes and Claude Baily were in the Shop. That was on the Wednesday. During the next couple of days I asked my boss and another fellow to help me split the weld and get it out. But they were too scared to touch it. Finally, it got to the Friday and they'd got the suspension on and the engine was in. So I got a fitter and apprentice to come back at eight o'clock. We chiselled the weld off and drilled out the rivets.

'We got 18 drawings out, plus the hammer, a pair of Gilbow snips, a protractor, and so on!

'We couldn't weld it up again, and Heynes came in on the Saturday morning. You couldn't see anything bar the weld had been cut.

' "Morning Bill," he said, "how's the car going? Has it been welded?"

' "Well," I replied, "it had been, but . . . it's going to be re-welded."

' "Oh! Did you find the hammer?"

' "Yes," I said, "and 18 drawings, a pair of snips, a . . . ." '

––––––––––

NORMAN DEWIS's daily testing logs – extracts

[Norman Dewis was Jaguar's chief test driver from 1952 until his retirement in the mid-eighties.]

5.06.52	*XK120C No. 11 Le Mans car. Run along by-pass, 6 stops from 100 mph . . . Fit latest type header tank.*
6.06.52	*XK120C No. 1 – Testing disc brakes.*
27.09.52	*Trip to Belgium for Motor road test [XK120C] and speed test Jabbeke road. Car driven to Dover. Breakfast 3/6 [17p], boat fare £1 16s 0d [£1.80], soap hotel 20F.*
15.11.52	*Blue Destruction Mark VII – bottom rubbers broken after 36 pavé miles, N/R split pin sheared on damper mounting peg, top dust cap broken, all rubbers broken and fatigued, leak in brake system. Plasticine gauge fitted to record flexibility of engine mounting.*
18.11.52	*Short road test on Mark VII, LWK 173, to be prepared for Scotland Yard.*
20.11.52	*Test at Lindley on Production XK120C No. 030.*
24.11.52	*General road test on XK120 Drop Head Coupe MHP 494.*
25.11.52	*Road test on XK120 Mark III.*
27.11.52	*Re-test of Production XK120C engine only. Engine frozen at dockside.*
27.11.52	*Sump cavitation test on XK120C 011.*
28.11.52	*Steering test on Mark VI 120 Fixed Head Coupe. [This is probably an error and should read, Mark IV – P.H.P.]*
9.12.52	*Cavitation test at Lindley on XK120C 001.*
10.12.52	*XK120C – production test at Lindley on chassis No. 032.*
22.12.52	*Short run on Mr. Lyons's Mark VII LDU 268, investigation into vibration. Suspect faulty axle. Short test on Holden Australian car. Excessive lost movement in steering. Exhaust booms. Clutch (heavy spring). Steering and driving position very poor. Damping and suspension very hard.*
5.01.53	*Test run on Mark VII high waistline car.*
15.01.53	*XK120C head taken to Leamington station for delivery to Weslake.*
22.01.53	*Steering test with R. Knight on XK120 Mark III. Investigation into oversteer.*
26.01.53	*Collected blue 2 seater from Dunlops, HKV 455.*
8.02.53	*Trip to Boy's High School at Uppingham with Mr. Heynes – XK120C 012.*
27.02.53	*Short road test on XK120C 001. 1952 Le Mans type rad layout. Dunlop disc brakes.*
16.03.53	*XK120C 001 – taken to Silverstone for Dunlop disc brake test. Car driven by T. Rolt, D. Hamilton, P. Walker. Club circuit used, 1.608 per lap. Best time put up by T. Rolt, 1m 18 secs. Brake fluid boiling every 10 laps approx. Water loss – 6 pints every 18 laps.*
30.03.53	*Start of journey to Belgium. Boat from Dover to Ostend, drove on to Bruges, arrived 8.0 approx. Hotel St. Sherbet.*
31.03.53	*Trial and testing all 3 cars on the Jabbeke road.*
1.04.53	*Operation Day. All records broken. The Mark VII gave marvellous results. The XK120C very disappointing. Revs 5800 max. Cars used: Mark VII LWK 343, 120 ex J. Claes, 120C 012.*
15.04.53	*Mr. Lyons's 2 seater special [Brontosauraus – P.H.P.] tested on the by-pass. 100 mph reached on the speedo (5100 rpm) . . . steering satisfactory, ride shade hard, insufficient cooling to exhaust silencer . . . reduce metal screen cowl, N/S tyre fouls wing valance on lock, transmission vibration at 5000 rpm, overrun very bad, gearchange very stiff. Bonnet prop rattles on bonnet. Give clutch pedal more clearance. Battery insecurely fastened. Suggest spring attachments for quick release of wing valances.*

Jaguar subsidiary companies in 1965
Jaguar Export Sales Ltd
The Lanchester Motor Company Ltd
Barker & Co. (Coachbuilders) Ltd
Guy Motors Ltd
Coventry Climax Engines Ltd
Coventry Climax Electrics Ltd
Newtherm Oil Burners Ltd
Jaguar Cars Inc
Jaguar-Daimler Distributors Inc
The Daimler Company Ltd
Transport Vehicles (Daimler) Ltd
Hooper & Co. (Coachbuilders) Ltd
Sunbeam Trolleybus Company Ltd
Coventry Diesel Engines Ltd
Henry Meadows Ltd
Badalini Transmissions Ltd (50%)
Jaguar Cars (Canada) Ltd
Jaguar of New York, Inc
Coventry Climax Engines (Australia) Pty Ltd
(The above are wholly owned unless otherwise stated)

C-type Jaguar, ex-Duncan Hamilton, OVC 915, completely reconditioned by Jaguars. Standing quarter 12.68, standing kilo 23.36. First offer over £2000.

November 1965

E-type fully prepared and modified to Group III racing. Many places this year, superb road car. Family commitments force sale. Ridiculous price £850.
XK120, 3.8, alloy body, D/head cams, discs all round, limited slip, c/r box. On SUs at moment, as used on road only. Haggling starts £400.
Practice car from 1953 Le Mans. XKC 038 works car, recently overhauled at Jaguars, 285 bhp, £2000 including all spares.

October 1966

30.04.53	Testing multi-plate clutch on XK120 Mark III.
7.05.53	Practice day at Silverstone. Cars running very well. Moss turned car over, bodywork badly damaged, otherwise car O.K. Best lap times: Moss – 1m 57 secs = 90.06 mph, Rolt – 1m 58 secs, Walker – 2m 2 secs.
18.05.53	Quiet day in shop.
20.05.53	XK120C 012 – Testing at Lindley Weber carbs with J. Emerson.
19.09.53	Prepared the Lyons special for drag tests at Gaydon.
20.09.53	Drag tests on the Lyons special completed at Gaydon. Cockpit needs enclosing more.
7.12.53	Tested Earl Howe Mark VII.
4.01.54	Testing at Silverstone with S. Moss. Cars used – 120C 011 and 120C Light Alloy car.
3.03.54	Strapping additional anti-roll bar to Baily's Mark VII. Continuation of high speed test on high waistline Mark VII. Slight prang on banking. Slid off banking due to snow patch, front of car clouting the wire safety fence – very effective.
4.03.54	Short test run with Mr. Heynes on Mark VII C-type [presumably a Mark VII fitted with a C-type head – P.H.P.]
3.04.54	XKD 401 – first test at Lindley. Engine misfiring and banging, returned to works. 15 laps on banking.
9.10.54	Testing with Wally, Black 2¹/₂ litre No.1 for rattles at rear.
24.10.54	Press day at Goodwood. Car used OKV 3. Clutch pedal faulty. Battery u/s.
1.12.54	Running Comp. Dept. XK120D with manual operated blind over radiator.
21.12.54	Pavé testing 2¹/₂ litre No.1 with Girling dampers fitted. 42 pave miles. Two small cracks in front crossmember. Steering very heavy on both locks. Several cracks around rear body members at road spring eye fixings. Car unfit for further pave work.
26.01.55 to 1.02.55 Endurance test on petrol injection.	
14.03.55	B.B.C. recording made for Alan Dixon. Car used XK120D OVC 501.
12.03.55	Testing 3 litre Ferrari at Lindley. Gearbox very noisy, whines and chatters, gears difficult to select. Engine very noisy and rough. Steering very heavy unless overdone on corners, then goes light. Cornering very good, rear end holds the corner with no sign of breakaway. If anything the front would go first. Oversteer very prominent. Brakes – very hard pedal. Suspect early fade. Engine vibration. Ride very hard. No kick in steering. Driving position very good, also visibility very good. 120 mph max on straight.
28.03.55	Short run on Merc 220 Saloon with R.J.K. [Bob Knight]
3.04.55	Testing 1st Production XK120D.
17/	Deliver Mercedes 220 over to France. Return with Duke of
18.04.55	Sutherland's Mark VII.
27.04.55	Testing OVC 501 and Comp "D" for tyres and handling. Hawthorn driving.
8.11.56	3.4 No. 2. Belgian test car. 127 mph at 4600 rpm.
17.11.56	Testing I.R.S. on D-type (swing axle).
30.11.56	Running petrol injection D-type for Shell film.
4.12.56	XK140 PRW 477 – run to Bletchley. Wrong day!!
5.12.56	Testing at Bletchley with XK140. Dynanometer again broke down at 140 mph.
1.01.57	Short road test on XK150.
18.01.57	Running XK150. Bonnet opened at 104 mph!!! Roof badly dented, bonnet wrecked.
11.02.57	Factory fire.
18.02.57	Performance test on 300SL Mercedes. The performance is not as good now that MIRA have returned the engine as were the previous tests. Also seems heavy on consumption. Gearbox –

difficult to engage gears.

1.03.57   *Testing Sebring D-type with 3.8 engine; engine misfiring at 4500 rpm. Brake pipe broke on rear caliper at 150 mph!!*

5.03.57   *Drag test on 300SL. 62 hp required for 100 mph. 2.4 Borg-Warner performance test – very poor indeed.*

18.03.57   *XKSS 401 – Lucas wiper test at MIRA.*

19.03.57   *D-type OVC 501 – transmission brake: complete failure.*

21.03.57   *XK140 B/W Coupe – disc brake test with 5th set of 113/B – batch cooked.*
            2.4 B/W – consumption test Birmingham traffic.

24.03.57   *3.4 Convertible – scuttle has sideways movement, shakes steering column very badly. Suggest inspection.*

1.04.57   *XKSS test – scavenge pump broken! Ex nut in engine.*

2.04.57   *Duke of Edinburgh's visit to MIRA.*

16.04.57   *XKSS – performance test with C. Hayward of the Autocar. Figures quite reasonable.*

24.05.57   *Running 3.4 on demonstration to Swiss journalists.*
            Running E-type at MIRA.
            Running Ecosse Jag at MIRA. 40 mph gale blowing.

12.06.57   *Hamilton "D" for Le Mans – gearbox seized.*

27.06.57   *Running D-type I.R.S.*

2.06.57   *Short run on integral Mark VII. Road test on 3.4 No. 1.*

9.09.57   *MIRA – running 3.4 Bueb Silverstone car, also Belgium D-type.*

6.02.59   *Road test on production 2.4 for Scotland Yard.*

19.03.59   *Silverstone – Dunlop tyre tests. Circuit very wet. J. Sears driving Austin Healey with Dunlop Duroband. The 150 lapped the Healey in 10 laps.*

24.03.59   *Comparison and handling tests – Dunlop RS4 versus Avon. Test to Southam and back (wet surface) using R.J.K. 2.4 Road noise: Dunlop best. Cornering: Avon has less understeer. Wander: less on Avon. Braking: Dunlop best. Ride: Dunlop best. Tyre squeal: same.*

27.03.59   *Cleaning office after re-paint. Testing special Dunlop spare wheel on 3.4 No. 2 car.*

2.04.59   *Mark IX Ministry of Supply car road tested.*

9.04.59   *Silverstone – Dunlop tyre tests. Aston Martin Grand Prix car there, Salvadori driving. Best lap time 1.46. 65 laps completed by the XK150. Best lap time 2.5.*

14.04.59   *Testing Service D-type. Short road test on Mark VII with air suspension. Brakes very poor.*

27.04.59   *Foot brake test on Oldsmobile on MIRA test hill.*

8.05.59   *MIRA – Maximum speed test on XK150 "S". Timed through lights at 126.7 mph (4700 rpm). Reaching 131 mph (5000 rpm) at end of straight.*

25.05.59   *Writing report on Mercedes 220 SE.*

12.06.59   *Running Ecosse D-type at MIRA.*

30.06.59   *Solex tests on Sir William's 2.4 MIRA – M.P.'s visiting day. 3.4 banking.*

2.07.59   *Running Service XKSS, argument with Italian customer re. engine pick up.*

26.08.59   *MIRA – testing both Tour de France cars.*

9.09.59   *Testing speaker system on Sir W. Lyons's Mark IX. Demonstrating Merc 220 SE to Borg-Warner rep.*

15.10.59   *Testing 3.8 Mark II Show demonstration car for Earls Court.*

8.12.59   *Road test on production 3.8 Mark II for the Aga Khan.*

21.01.60   *Road test on Billy Cotton's 3.8 Mark II, report handed to F.R. England.*

23.02.60   *Running E-type No.3, R.J. Knight, Rheese, Palmer observing, inside front wheel lifting 1 1/2" approx.*

25.02.60   *Body noise and vibration tests with R.J.K. Mercedes, 3.8 Mark*

	II, I.R.S. Mark II tested. Sir W. Lyons present. 3.8 Mark II gave best results.
29.02.60	First run on Competition E-type [E2A]. Not very impressive at this stage. Meeting with Cunningham, Hansgen & Momo.
9.03.60	Short road test on Rolls Bentley.
22.03.60	Meeting with all production supervisors and personnel to go over and sort out 3.4 production car. Improvements will be made to ensure a better quality car. Conversation with Sir W. Lyons re. production.
22.04.60	Film work with World Wide Pictures (XDU 984).
30.05.60	Running Aston Martin DB4. Steering niggle. Axle whine – 70 mph (bad). Ride shade hard. Some shake. Backlash in diff unit – wind up. Car understeers. Steering direct and positive. Seating and pedal layout very good. Visibility good. Gear selector good. Some gearbox noise overrun. Exhaust note reasonable. Storm noise reasonable. Engine layout and finish good. Squeak from water pump.
15.06.60	MIRA – members and press Open Day. 3.8 Mark II banking. 132 laps (396 people as passengers).
16.06.60	Blue E-type – Dunlop tyre tests M1 motorway.
29.06.60	Short test on Daimler Dart V8 SP 250. Very bad scuttle shake. Steering has no self-centring when cornering. Engine performance not impressive. General finish of car very poor.
4.07.60	MIRA – performance test on Daimler Majestic Major V8 4.6 litre. Figures identical to Mark IX 3.8. Heavy judder on drive away – engine mountings. Steering has strong castor feel, front tyres squeal readily when cornering.
29.05.61	E-type pavé testing – bonnet fitted having bonded diaphragm brackets in place of spot welds.
18.07.61	E-type water splash test – 10 leaks.

This 'leaping Jaguar' is an XJ6 prototype undergoing development testing.

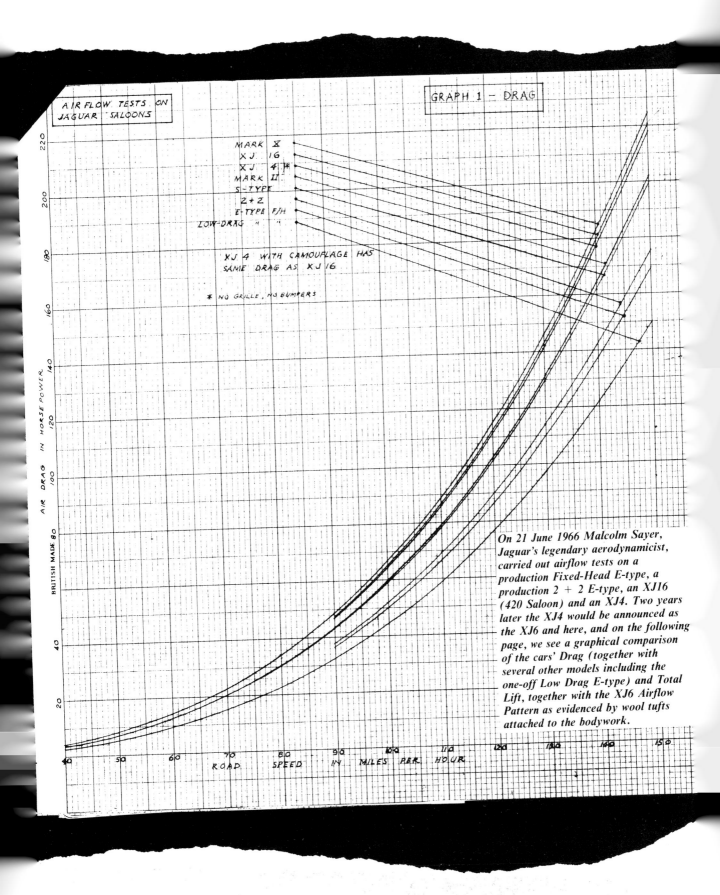

AIR FLOW TESTS ON JAGUAR SALOONS

GRAPH 1 - DRAG

MARK X
XJ 16
XJ 4 *
MARK II
S-TYPE
2+2
E-TYPE F/H
LOW-DRAG " "

XJ 4 WITH CAMOUFLAGE HAS SAME DRAG AS XJ 16

* NO GRILLE, NO BUMPERS

AIR DRAG IN HORSE POWER

BRITISH MADE

ROAD SPEED IN MILES PER HOUR

On 21 June 1966 Malcolm Sayer, Jaguar's legendary aerodynamicist, carried out airflow tests on a production Fixed-Head E-type, a production 2 + 2 E-type, an XJ16 (420 Saloon) and an XJ4. Two years later the XJ4 would be announced as the XJ6 and here, and on the following page, we see a graphical comparison of the cars' Drag (together with several other models including the one-off Low Drag E-type) and Total Lift, together with the XJ6 Airflow Pattern as evidenced by wool tufts attached to the bodywork.

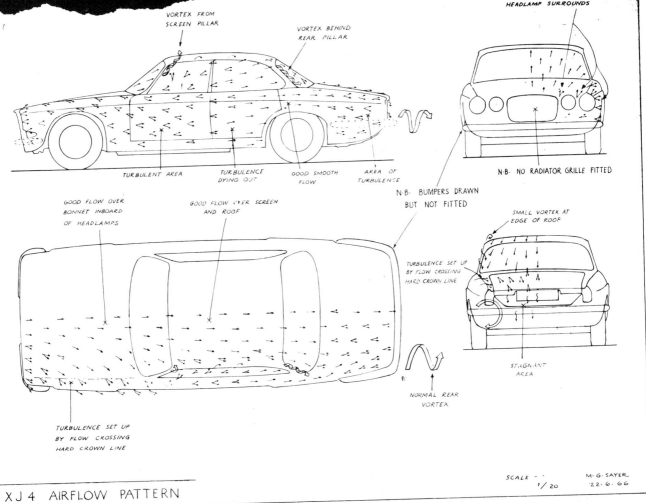

XJ4 AIRFLOW PATTERN

SCALE -- 1/20   M.G. SAYER 22.6.66

24th June 1966

From M.G. SAYER   To MR. W.M. HEYNES
Copies to: Sir William Lyons, Mr. Knight, Mr. Thornton, Mr. Croft
WINDTUNNEL TESTS OF VARIOUS JAGUAR SALOONS
Tests were made at MIRA on June 21st 1966 on a production Fixed
Head E-type, a production 2 + 2, an XJ16 and an XJ4 with and without
camouflage. The XJ4 also lacked a radiator grille and bumpers.

In each case drag and lift were measured and wool-tuft behaviour
was observed in the case of XJ16 and XJ4.

Results are compared with previous tests made by MIRA on Mark
X, Mark II and S-type.

SUMMARY OF RESULTS

| Model | DRAG/HP at 100 mph | LIFT (lb) at 100 mph | |
		FRONT	REAR
E-type	50.17	84.0	82.2
2 + 2	52.01	76.9	86.8
S-type	58.97	-	-
Mark II	59.87	-	-
XJ4	64.63	212.0	63.4
XJ4 + Camouflage	65.19	188.1	51.7
XJ16	65.30	158.2	99.0
Mark X	66.57	-	-

NOTES ON RESULTS:

1. XJ4.

(A) Airflow pattern – see diagram. The hard crown lines of the wings,
coupled with the rather abrupt change of curvature above and beside the
headlamps, caused a large area of turbulence on the side of the car,
extending to halfway along the rear door. This would have the effect of
increasing drag and possibly giving rise to buffeting wind noise on the
windows as compared with a more rounded front such as a Mark II.
However, it is characteristic of most cars having the more angular modern
lines.

The effect of hard crown lines was demonstrated by the performance of
the car when fitted with camouflage. This gave the front wings a rounded
top, by padding, and despite very sharp rectangular front and rear ends, the
drag of the car rose by less than 1%.

(B) Drag. The high drag recorded was largely due to the turbulence
described above but may be reduced by the following:-

a)   Fitting a radiator grille should reduce the volume of air passing into the
bonnet.

b)   Fitting a front bumper may reduce the drag induced by frontal lift and
may also help to smooth the flow along the lower part of the side.

c)   It may be found possible to improve conditions at the front of the car
below bumper level once tests have been made with the bumper fitted.

(C) Lift. The frontal lift was very high, and unless this is found to decrease
considerably when bumper and grille are fitted, stability at high speeds will
be difficult to achieve. It must also be borne in mind that lift figures from
MIRA have not always been reliable, and a dimensional check on lift
experienced on the track would be reassuring.

2. XJ16

(A) Airflow pattern. The new front had almost identical characteristics to
the XJ4 (q.v.) except that the presence of the bumper smoothed out the flow
over the lower part of the side. The area of turbulence on the side extended
some 18 inches further back than on the S-type.

(B) Drag. This was 11% higher than the S type, mostly because of the
turbulence already described, but partly due to the larger intake for the
improved cooling system.

(C) Lift. Total lift was lower than for the XJ4 and it was more evenly
distributed with 66% on the front axle compared with 77% for the XJ4.
Unfortunately, MIRA could not provide reliable lift figures for the E-type
for comparison.

Extract from the Chairman's Statement at the Annual General Meeting held on 25 February 1966

'In this year our car production would have reached an all-time record, exceeding the previous figure by a considerable margin, had it not been for the fact that, in June, we suffered an unconstitutional strike of five weeks duration. The effect of this strike on our profits was considerable, particularly as it came at a time when we were enjoying the highest rate of production that we had ever achieved. Over £5 million in turnover was lost by Jaguar as a result of this and the unconstitutional strikes at certain of our suppliers, and it is perhaps appropriate that I should mention that £600,000 was lost in wages by our employees. There is no doubt that, had we been able to maintain full production, our profits would have reflected favourably the increased capacity which has been brought into use during the year.

'We continue to be concerned by the very considerable rise in costs, mainly outside our control, which we are called upon to absorb, represented by increases in production materials and wages, and in almost every element of establishment charges. Unfortunately, there is no evidence of these costs becoming stable in the near future.

'In my view there is no doubt that until we can establish in this country an effective control of wages relative to productivity, which I do not believe can be achieved by any voluntary system, the competitive position of the country must be insecure.

'However, there is to be found considerable encouragement in the fact that, in the main, the heads of our Unions now recognise the need for establishing discipline within their ranks. We must hope that this will lead to some integration between Unions, and the introduction of some system of penalties which will enforce compliance with the Procedure System laid down in the National Agreements.

'Unfortunately, there is still a belief amongst some of the highest Government and Union circles that strikes are less prevalent here than in other countries, and statements to this

The front cover of the sales brochure which introduced the XJ6 to the British motoring public.

effect make no contribution towards bringing home the fact that we cannot afford them if we are to stay in business successfully. I believe it to be true that, whilst the number of official strikes may be less in other countries, our total of unconstitutional strikes is vastly greater.

Cars of interest that were, at various times, under the control of the Experimental Department, together with their fate in some instances (as stated on Company paperwork)

'I would summarise the position by saying that with modern, well-equipped factories and an established and very successful range of cars at our disposal, we are in a very competitive position. I hope the day will not be too long delayed when I can safely state that we and the industry as a whole have resolved satisfactorily the two major factors endangering our future livelihood – rising costs and unconstitutional stoppages of work. A solution to both must be found before the Company and its employees can be assured finally of the prosperity for which we strive and which we know can be achieved.'

W. LYONS

COMPETITION CARS

	XKC 201	Green – being reduced to produce
	XKC 301	Green – enveloping body design, being reduced to produce by Service Dept.
OVC 1	XKD 401	BRG – on loan to Montagu Motor Museum
OKV 1	XKD 402	Green – sold
OKV 2	XKD 403	Green – sold
	XKD 505	BRG – sold
	XKD 506	Cream and Blue; body only – scrapped
	XKD 601	Cream and Blue; Briggs Cunningham – scrapped
	XKD 605	BRG – on loan to Turin museum
	No chassis No.	Fibre-glass body – scrapped

XK TYPES

HKV 455	660001	On loan to Dunlop (crashed) – reduced to produce by Service Dept
JWK 675	670172	Blue – written-off whilst on loan to Dunlops
MHP 494	667001	Black Drop Head Coupe – last used by Mr J. Lyons
	804001	Black Hard-top – recently reduced to produce
	804004	Blue Hard-top – sold

XK150

	No chassis No.	Pearl Grey FHC – reduced to Produce
No. 1	S837003	Red – sold to Mike Hawthorn

MARK VII/VIII/XI

	710002	Black	High Waist Line Body
	No chassis No.	Black	Integral construction Scrapped
KRW 621	710006	B.R. Green	Light Alloy Body Sold to R. Berry
	750001		Drop Head Coupe Reduced to Produce
	750002		Drop Head Coupe Reduced to Produce
LHP 3	710177	Battleship Grey	On loan (?) to Mr Weslake
MKV 617	713757	Green	Sold to Duncan Hamilton
	727554 BW		Unfinished car intended for Queen Mother
SWK 280	75052 DN		3.8 L 9:1 engine

2.4 LITRE SALOONS

	900001	Black	
	900002	Birch Grey	Reduced to Produce
	900003	Pastel Blue	Reduced to Produce
	900004	Battleship Grey	Sold
	900005	B.R. Green	Reduced to Produce
	900006	Suede Green	Reduced to Produce
	900009	Pearl Grey	Sold to Mr Whittaker
	900019	White	Pavé Test Car Reduced to Produce
	908558	Pearl Grey	Wrap-Round Windscreen Scrapped

YDU 294	976913	B.R. Green	SU carburettors
SWK 765	970690 BW	B.R. Green	SP 250 engine
	120852	Warwick Grey	3 L engine fitted

3.4 AND 3.8 LITRE SALOONS

No.1	No chassis No.	Pastel Green	Reduced to Produce
No.2	900163	Battleship Grey	Sold to Dunlop
No.3	No chassis No.	Battleship Grey	IRS Reduced to Produce
TVC 420	S970095 DN	Sherwood Green	Light alloy doors, etc Sold to R. Blake
	S970690 DN	B.R. Green	On loan to Dunlop Light alloy doors, etc Air suspension SP 250 engine Sold
	No chassis No.	Black	Convertible F. Gardener's dept. Reduced to Produce
Body No.	E004182	Black	Wide Rear Track Fuel Injection IRS Reduced to Produce
	975760	Cotswold Blue	P.A. Steering
	976913	B.R. Green	Competition type
	993346	Pastel Blue	Competition type
	978688	Carmine (?) Red	Competition type
5861 HP	201300	Battleship Grey	Specially welded body Sold
1 off Mk II body shell		Unpainted	Not numbered (For modification to GT type)
	104892	B.R.G.	Restyled boot, etc
	213291	Cotswold Blue	Air conditioning
	207515	B.R.G.	Estate Car
Mark III No.1 Exp III/1		Gunmetal	IRS Borg-Warner (proto S-type) Scrapped
Mark III No.2 Exp III/2		Birch Grey	IRS Manual gearbox
	210002 BW	Cotswold Blue	3 carburettor mock-up

E-TYPE

VKV 752	No.1	Pastel Green	returned to Produce
	No.2	Pearl Grey	Returned to Produce
	No.3	Unpainted	Scrapped
	No.4	Cotswold Blue	Fuel Injection Returned to Produce
	No.5	Red	Corvette Gearbox Scrapped
	No.6	Metallic Grey	FHC Low roof line Scrapped
9600 HP	No.7	Metallic Grey	FHC Press Car Sold
	875001	Mist Grey	Pave Test Car Dismantled

	885007	Bronze	Scrapped
4133 RW	850025	B.R.G.	3 L engine
			5 speed gearbox

XJ8 (2 + 2)

No.1	1E 50001	Sand	Scrapped
No.3		Pearl	Crash Test Scrapped

MARK X

	No.1	Black	Daimler engine
	302485 BW	B.R.G.	Lightweight Body

MARK II

3339 KV	1B 50010 BW	B.R.G.	4.2 L engine

XJ5

No.4	ID 50003 DN	White	Prepared to receive V12
No.5	ID 50002 DN	Sand	V12 engine

DAIMLER SECTION

1902 HP	100666	Red Hard top	SP 250 Sold
	100571	Green Hard top	SP 250 Sold
	100003	Black	SP 252 Restyled
	100004	Maroon	SP 252 Restyled

In 1968 the former Jaguar Cars Inc., became one of three divisions of British Leyland Motors Inc., and Eerdmans, who was approaching retirement, stood down and proposed Graham Whitehead as President of the newly-formed company. Today Whitehead is in charge of Jaguar's US operations. (Jaguar Cars US)

121

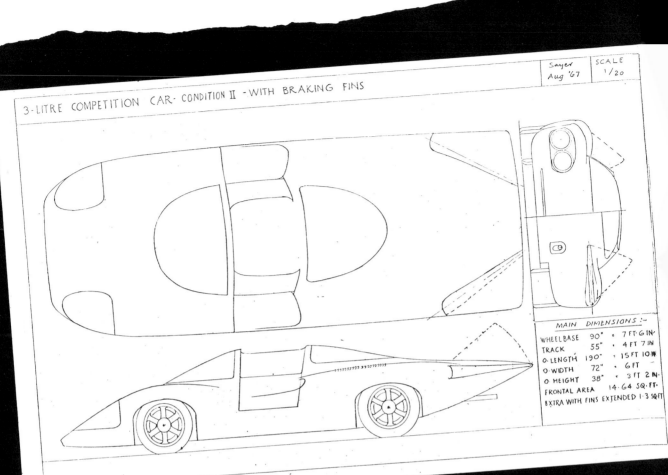

Sayer
Aug '67

SCALE
1/20

3-LITRE COMPETITION CAR· CONDITION II -WITH BRAKING FINS

MAIN DIMENSIONS :-
WHEELBASE   90"   = 7 FT· 6 IN·
TRACK   55"   = 4 FT 7 IN
O· LENGTH   190"   = 15 FT 10 IN
O· WIDTH   72"   = 6 FT
O· HEIGHT   38"   = 3 FT 2 IN·
FRONTAL AREA   14·64 SQ·FT·
EXTRA WITH FINS EXTENDED 1·3 SQ·FT

LOFTY ENGLAND

In late 1967 Malcolm Sayers designed three more mid-engined sports racing cars with a view to following up his XJ13 design. Of these three, the one described as 'Condition II' had the novel idea of 'braking fins'. An airbrake had been used, of course, by Mercedes-Benz on the 300 SLR at Le Mans in 1955 when attempting to combat the effectiveness of the D-type's disc brakes.

In the early sixties Jaguar's entire engineering and development division comprised just 30 people.

Warren Pearce face to face with the opposition at Crystal Palace in 1967. (Laurence Pearce)

'Sir William drove everything we made, including the Brontosaurus. I remember him belting round the factory in it!'

'I first met Michael MacDowel in 1959 when Lister were running at Le Mans with 3-litre Jaguar engines we loaned to them – which unfortunately proved a bit unsatisfactory inasmuch as all the titanium connecting rods broke – and he was then their reserve driver. A very quiet, unassuming, nice bloke, who just stepped in when asked to and went as fast as anybody alse.

'At that time, he was doing a short service commission as an engineering officer in the RAF. Some little time afterwards he wrote to me and said that he was finishing his commission and he wondered if there was any job for him in Jaguar Cars.

'In actual fact, we wanted someone in the Service Department so I offered him a typical Jaguar job: You worked seven days a week, 24 hours a day, for nothing!

'By then I'd been elevated to Assistant Managing Director. We weren't racing ourselves then, of course, but I got him to take over the competition activities. He was responsible for all the Tour de France successes with Consten; he and Ted Brookes.

'Then we launched the E-type in '61 and the first few cars we delivered, I had arranged to be delivered to people who might do some good with them, which included Coombs, Sopwith, McLaren and one or two people like that. So MacDowel became involved in that and then it went through the stages of being upgraded to the first Lightweight "E" that we did and which Coombs ran. So MacDowel got to know Coombs very well.

'About '63 MacDowel talked to me about John Coombs having offered him a job as General Manager. So I said, "Oh yes, but you do realise that the average life of a General Manager at Coombs of Guildford is something like three months". John always fell out with them.

'Coombs came to me, quite rightly, and asked if I was prepared to release him. So I said, "To do what and for how much?"

'He said it was to be General Manager, and at three times the salary I was paying him! I couldn't really foresee that he was going to get that for a long time at Jaguar, unless he took my job. So I said to MacDowel, "You go ahead. You're sticking your neck out, but if you can stick it out, you're home and dry."

'On a couple of occasions I had to go down and give him a pep talk. Anyway they got on very well, and later in the piece Coombs provided him with his hillclimb cars in which he became British Hillclimb Champion.'

John Coombs has now retired and lives in Monaco. Michael MacDowel became Managing Director many years ago, though sadly due to British Leyland, this famous and very successful garage is no longer a Jaguar dealership.

'Jackie Stewart introduced me recently as the first man who gave him a works drive.

'I said, "That's not quite true, Jackie".

'"Well," he said, "the first works-supported drive."

'That's quite true. His first works-supported drive, in effect, was with Coombs in the Lightweight "E".'

In March 1967 a sheet of performance figures for the Jaguar saloon cars, Rover 2000TC and Mercedes-Benz 250S and 250SE models was prepared and sent to Messrs Whittaker, Heynes, England, Hassan, Knight, and Mundy with an information copy to Sir William Lyons. Attached to the report was a memo which stated the following.

'The performance figures for the 2.4-litre saloon are those of the Mark I model since no Mark 2 version has been tested. This is due to the fact that, despite very serious investigations, it has never proved possible to produce a 2.4-litre Mark 2 saloon with a performance in line with that of the Mark I.'

ON THE FACTORY FIRE

'The only thing that kept the whole damn place from going up was the cars hanging from the roof. We were just changing from the 140 to the 150 and in those days we always used to keep a few bodies-in-white, complete shells. So the easiest thing was to hang them down from the roof girders.

'At that time there were no sprinklers and none of the release panels that automatically open and let out the fire. We hadn't done any of that 'cause it was a wartime building, and the underside of the corrugated iron roof was bitumastic painted, which doesn't half go!

'I was there when this happened. We had 16 fire brigades and it was a roaring furnace. The only thing that saved it was that the whole roof structure got so hot the weight of these bodies pulled the roof girders down, and the fire went out of the top. Otherwise, they weren't stopping it.

'My office was on the right-hand side by the Service entrance. We lost the Service Department and it got to the point where I didn't think I was going to have any records. So I moved all my records out of my office over the road to a little cafe place we used to have.'
I asked Lofty how it had started.

'Nobody's very sure. There was the Service Department and the Saw Mill, and a press board wall between them, and for some reason that got on fire – whether it was a cigarette or what, I don't know. Nearby was the tyre stock and that got on fire, and that got the roof on fire, which was bitumastic, and in five minutes it was neither here nor there.

'As it happened, it was just the moment we were launching the 3.4 Mark II with automatic transmission, and we had a modification on it. They were all round the building!

'It was six o' clock in the evening and there were only about 20 or 30 people there. So we had to get all these bods: "Driven an automatic?"
' "No!"
' "Get in! Don't worry about. Get the hell out of it". And they just drove them away and stuck them anywhere, on the road or anywhere.

'The lucky thing was that it didn't get to the paintshop which was nearby. If it had got through to there, we'd have had it. But we didn't lose anything that wasn't easily replaceable, fortunately. The cars didn't matter. Everybody pulled together and was wonderful. We only lost two days production.

'Dunlop, who had bought our old factory at Foleshill, had extended it but they said, "We haven't moved in yet, so you move in". So we moved the test and rectification to Dunlop, and we had a new building – 100,000 square feet or something – put up in 13 weeks from the word go. Wonderful, the help was fabulous.

'So production went up, instead of down! Successful fire!'

ON THE JAGUAR/LOTUS CONNECTION

'We were one of the first people to use monocoque construction, and I remember Bill Heynes talked Colin Chapman into going monocoque. He was a good friend of ours. Colin was at Silverstone once and tried our car soon after he got started.

'We bought Lotus.

'Old Sir William was no fool. The most important thing is the engineering. If you haven't got the right engineers, you needn't even start. He felt it was no good waiting till Heynes retired, he wanted some bright boys to follow on. So he tried talking to John Cooper and he was quite impressed with Cooper, but they'd got their own business and they didn't want to know.

'Then he talked to Gordini – good firm, very good. He and I went to see Gordini when we were in Paris.

'Then one day Chapman came up in conversation. I was Chairman of the Motor Sport Committee and so came across him. At that time he was down at Hackney underneath the railway arches, so I arranged to go and see him. Graham Hill was then working for him as a mechanic.

'So I took Chapman out to lunch and suggested that he might like to come in with us. "No," he said, "I've got this far on my own. I'm scratching through at the moment so I'd like to carry on." Fair enough.

'Then he got to the Elan and by this time he'd moved out to Cheshunt. I was still seeing him and he mentioned he was having a lot of trouble with the body of the Elan and the paint bubbling up when it got hot. So I said, "Look, we had exactly the same trouble with the SP250. We've put it all right. So bring your blokes up and we'll tell you anything you want to know".

'So he does this and then he said, "What about coming to see my place". So I went down. It was one of these modern industrial units, not very big – not bad.

'When I got back I said to Sir William, "I reckon we could buy this lot for £1/2 million, complete with the motor racing side". He said he'd better have a look at it, so I took him down.

' "I think you're right," he said. So we then negotiated with Chapman and got to the point where they actually shook hands. It was a share deal. The Old Man then went off to South Africa, or somewhere, and about a week later a letter came from Chapman saying that they'd reconsidered this and would we be good enough to let them withdraw.

'So I thought to myself, "He's not coming in on the right foot if he doesn't want to do it". So I said, without asking the Old Man, "fair enough".

'I'm very glad I did. I can't imagine Colin Chapman and British Leyland, can you?'

CYRIL CROUCH, who joined the Company in 1948, on the two Mark VII convertibles that were made

'I had quite a lot of input on those.

'We had a screen in front and also some peculiar device I devised for the side windows. I had a cam arrangement and two shields came across. With the window down they snapped back into position and went down into the door. It had an hydraulic linkage on it and a driving system that was developed by an offshoot of Wilmot Breedon.

'There were two fully prepared cars. The reason we didn't go ahead with them was that there was a lot of scuttle shake, and we had to do a lot of reinforcing. We didn't have any assistance from the chassis itself, being a separate chassis, but the Old Man decided they looked pretty and were a good exercise. But then they were broken up, which was a great pity, and there were never any photographs taken of them.

'The linkage I did for the hood was very much along the theme of the big American cars. It was fully automatic – all you had to do was release two catches, press a button and the whole thing went down. The interior of the hood sticks were lined, and it was a very smart looking car.

'But the scuttle shake was considered to be too bad for a Jaguar.'

'We were then beginning to concentrate on the little car, the 2.4 as it came out. It started life built around a 2-litre, four-cylinder engine. Before it came out, we abandoned the four-cylinder engine and went for the 2.4, six-cylinder.

'This was the first unitary construction that we did, of course, and I designed the body, particularly the front end around the 2-litre, four-cylinder engine. It went to a 2.4, then a 3.4, then a 3.8 and then a

It was calculated, in the late sixties, that the Jaguar V8 engine was going to cost £132 2. 3. in material and £29. 0. 4. in labour.

4.2, still in the same body construction that I did around the four-cylinder!

'I once said to Bill Heynes, "Look, Mr Heynes, you remember that I did this body around a four-cylinder, 2-litre engine. Now you're talking about putting a 4.2-litre engine in it".

' "Oh, well Cyril, if you've done your job right, it'll be all right. By the way, this V12 engine we're beginning to look at – will that go in?"

' "No it won't!" I replied,' recalls Crouch with much mirth.

'Space has always been a problem with Jaguar. We couldn't fit automatic transmission to the E-type until we did the 2 + 2. We had the same problem with the old Mark I/II. When that started out, automatic gearboxes were still in their infancy.

'Bill Heynes asked me why I hadn't catered for the automatic gearbox on that model, and I replied that it wasn't even in existence when I did the tunnel.

'The next model came along and I said to him, "Are you going to put automatic transmission in this?"

' "No, I shouldn't bother with that. . . Where are you going?"

'I said, "I'm going to switch the tape recorder on!"

'Similar things happened with the XJ40. I asked if we were going to put the V12 engine in it. "No no," I was told, "we've got a power unit coming along which will do everything that the V12 does."

'I said I was pleased to hear that because we'd have a lighter motor car. Now, of course, they're trying madly to put the V12 in!'

ON OTHER PROJECTS

'Sir William started working on a little runabout, van-type body. This was the time when his son was given a sort of free hand, and he started to develop a lightweight, van-type thing.

'It never got to anything, but he had this thing built up. I don't think it ever went on the road – peculiar looking thing.

'The Old Man would play around with various shapes and projects – he was a ball of fire, of course, all the time. He'd have several projects going at the same time. He would take a current car and start to carve it up, see what he could make of it, realise it was a waste of time, stop that one and start to think about something else.'

I reminded Cyril of a small sports car that Norman Dewis had once mentioned to me was built in the mid-fifties.

'Yes, I remember that. I think that one did go on to the road. It was only a one-off again. I think Sir William decided we've got to earn some money somewhere.

'It hadn't got the revolutionary design or flair that Sir William produced with the XK120. It was the sort of size of a little MG at that time. It was a very small car, very low and had a separate chassis, which was bought in.'

ON THE DAIMLER SP250

'That was another acquisition, but it was like a bit of jelly on the road!

'I remember one Saturday morning, not long after we'd completed the purchase of Daimler, I went down with Bill Heynes and we got into one of these Daimler Darts. We went round this sort of perimeter track.

' "Good lord, Cyril. The first thing you've got to do is put some steel reinforcings in."

'Of course this was the time when they were very much involved in bus work, and they were doing a bit of armoured car work as well.

'I said, "What are you going to do with this, with the military stuff?"

' "Oh that's the only profitable thing that he's bloomin' bought, he says!"

'The Mark X wasn't a success really. The body was very heavy. Bill Heynes insisted on 16-gauge sill panels and so on. The heating distribution was pretty poor. It was too large for this country really, and it wasn't quick enough off the mark for the Americans. It was sluggish.

'The 4.2 engine made it a nice motor car, but by then it had got a name, and whatever we did to it, we couldn't do much of a rescue act on it.

'That was one of the non-successes of Jaguar – about the only one, I would think.'

'Then we did the 420 with a facelift on the front end, and the rear end. I think we ran out of ideas on how much further we could modify that car! So we had to start afresh on the XJ6.'

'There were six prototype XJ Coupes made, which had "M" registrations. Tom Jones wrapped his round a lamp post and wrote it off. I hit some parking meters and wrote mine off and Ted Willday's example rusted away. I don't think there are any of them left.

'There was a long delay in bringing them out because there was a production problem at Castle Bromwich. We were in the throes of introducing the long wheelbase, and that was eventually the reason why we dropped the thing. Overall we didn't make many because it didn't fit into the production run at Castle Bromwich. It needed a separate track.

'The Americans really instigated the model. They persuaded us to do a two-door, pillarless saloon. But the price we put it into America caused problems. They said that they didn't expect to pay more for a car like this. They expected to pay less for it than the normal sedan!

'They lost their initial enthusiasm for it and, with the production problems, we dropped it.'

'I've always been totally committed to everything body – from body-in-white to what I used to to call the last bit of rag trim we put on the floor.

'John Egan joined us and said, "Cyril, I wish you wouldn't call our expensive carpet and cloth, rag!"

'So I said, "Well John, you're new to the game. It's always been known as rag trim, and it always will be." '

In September 1968 Malcolm Sayer sent Sir William Lyons his first thoughts and sketches for a '2 + 2 sports car based on XJ4 parts'. This was the beginnings of the XJ-S and amongst the variety of designs put forward was this one.

A 3-litre production version of the XK engine was considered for production and was fitted in a Mark II saloon for assessment. Norman Dewis, the Chief Tester, was impressed as can be seen from his interesting conclusions.
(Norman Dewis)

In April 1967

The Mark II 2.4 with Ambla trim was costing £690 14. 9. to produce, and selling for £1341 10. 3. incl. Purchase Tax
The Mark II 2.4 with leather was costing £705 4. 6. to produce, and selling for £1393 11. 4. incl. Purchase Tax
The Mark II 3.8 was costing £726 15. 6$^{1/2}$. to produce, (Materials £605 4. 0$^{1/2}$./Labour £121 11. 6.) and selling for £1541 17. 4. incl. Purchase Tax
The XJ6 was estimated to cost £788 4. 5$^{1/2}$. to produce, (Materials £677 0. 10$^{1/2}$./Labour £111 3. 7.)
    'If the following items are deleted: Mouldings, Bonnet Pads, Rim bellishers, overriders, clock and the minimum amount of felts are used then a further saving of £12 0. 0. could be made.'

From: Mr. N. Dewis.   EXPERIMENTAL DEPARTMENT.

To: Mr. Hassan.   5th January 1968.
Copies to: Mr. Heynes, Mr. R.J. Knight,   EXP/2469/ND.
Mr. Mundy, Mr. Wilkinson.

3 LITRE ENGINE PERFORMANCE TESTS.

        Tests have now been completed on the Gold head and "Small inlet port" head which in turn have been performance tested on the 3 litre engine.

Vehicle:	Warwick Grey MK II.
Engine:	3 Litre No. E 1317 C.R. 9:1
Carbs:	Twin H.S.8.
Needles:	U.M.
Axle Ratio:	4.55:1 with Overdrive.
Fuel:	Shell Super.

ACCELERATION TOP GEAR	GOLD HEAD AV. SECS.	"SMALL INLET PORT". AV. SECS.
10 – 30 m.p.h.	6.18	6.1
20 – 40 "	5.9	6.0
30 – 50 "	6.0	6.2
40 – 60 "	6.4	6.3
50 – 70 "	6.3	6.3
60 – 80 "	6.7	6.9
70 – 90 "	7.1	7.7
80 – 100 "	8.2	8.8
90 – 110 "	12.7 O/D Gear.	13.3 O/D Gear.

REST TO IN GEARS		
0 – 30 m.p.h.	3.4	3.4
0 – 40 "	5.6	5.7
0 – 50 "	7.3	7.2
0 – 60 "	10.4	10.3
0 – 70 "	12.8	12.6
0 – 80 "	16.3	16.05
0 – 90 "	20.6	20.2
0 – 100 "	25.5	25.3
0 – 110 "	34.9	35.4
Standing ¼ mile	17.2	17.03

Max. through timing lights 118.7 m.p.h.)
Max. at the end of straight 122   m.p.h.

Weather Condition.

Atmos. Temp.	40°F	34°F
Wind.	Zero	S.W. Gusting 10 m.p.h.
Baro.	Instrument not recording.	

CONCLUSION.

        From the above results there is no performance gain in favour of the "small port head", I would therefore recommend we use the standard Gold Head.

        The general driveability and pick up is very good, also the engine is smooth and free from vibration periods throughout its speed range.

Contd....

For a 3 litre engine the performance figures are very impressive even allowing for the 4.55:1 axle ratio which is well suited with the overdrive which gives an overall ratio of 3.54:1.   It was possible to record 90 m.p.h. to 110 m.p.h. in normal top gear but the best timed figures for this speed range were recorded in overdrive.

I feel there is a wide interest for a good 3 litre engine for which this unit would be most promising.

The maximum speed of 122 m.p.h. recorded at M.I.R.A. is not the ultimate maximum that could be achieved given a longer straight than is available at M.I.R.A.

N. DEWIS.

XJS with camouflaged body-lines. Always controversial as a styling exercise, even some Jaguar-lovers might think this a positive improvement!

**BOB BETT, who for many years ran the advertising agency retained by
Jaguar Cars**

'It was my brother who started our business and he called it Nelson
Advertising. He had been with Henlys, the motor people, who were then
sponsoring Swallow Coachbuilding. When he started up his own
business, he did Henlys' advertising and started off with Swallow as one
of the firms we worked for. My brother started in 1928 and I joined him
in 1932. By that time, they had become S.S. Cars.

'My brother was very friendly with Bill Lyons personally and I
remember, in the first year I was there, doing our budget for S.S. Cars
which came to £1000 for a year – 13 pages in *The Autocar* and 13 pages
in *The Motor.*

'In 1935 they brought out a different version of the S.S. The first
ones had had the low-slung bodies and they had the nickname of the
"Sexy Six" or the "Sissy Six", or whatever. Apart from that S.S. was a
bad name in Europe at the time, with the Nazis being around.

'My brother decided that they should change the name from S.S.,
and Bill Lyons said, "All right, come up with some ideas," – which we
did.

'I, in fact, was the one who produced Jaguar. We had a few other
names because we wanted something you could get your teeth into, an
animal preferably, but a lot of them were taken up, and Jaguar happened
to be available, although it was used by Alvis for an aero-engine.

'Anyhow Bill Lyons didn't like it, but he was always a man who
wanted other people's views, including Bertie Henly, and a few others.
They were all against it, because they thought S.S. was a good name. My
brother spent two or three days in Coventry staying with Bill Lyons to
insist that we got this name, and he eventually agreed. So we then said
that we would call it the S.S. Jaguar, and we came back.

'The next day Bill Lyons phoned up my brother and said, "I've
changed my mind now".

'My brother, who was called Bill too, said, "You're too late. There's
an advertisement in tomorrow's *Daily Mail.*" And that was that!

'My brother really took a chance because we could have cancelled it,
but he was so insistent on it, and of course it was the best thing that ever
happened to them.

'Lyons didn't know much about finance. It was my brother who
promoted Jaguar to a public company. He had spent a year or two in the
City and got to know finance very well. When Bill Lyons wanted to go
public it was my brother who coped with it all for him. He had no
business feeling in that way at all.

'The reason for going public was to raise money. It was Henlys, of
course, who started him off and Bertie Henly always felt that. It was one
of the things that he did to help Lyons, and it was quite true.

'Bertie was a very able man and very shrewd.

'The worst thing that happened in racing was the disaster in 1955. I
was at Le Mans that year. Mike Hawthorn and Fangio were having a
colossal battle at a tremendous speed and they were just neck and neck. I
was in the pits when it happened and we didn't quite appreciate how bad
it was.

'Lofty, who was in charge of the pits, called Hawthorn in and Mike
was very distressed and he didn't want to drive any longer. But Lofty
insisted, "Mike, you're going out again".

'Then the Mercedes built up a lead and pulled out, to everyone's
astonishment at about two o'clock in the morning. Then Jaguar won the
race and it was called a hollow victory, which it was in a way. But it
didn't mean to say, in my opinion, that they wouldn't have won.

'At the time we had all agreed that, whoever won, we would advertise the race. But when I came back and saw the headlines in the *Daily Express*, "Disaster at Le Mans", I changed my mind a bit.

'Next morning, I got in the office a bit quick. Bill Lyons was on to me very early on and asked me what I thought about the matter. I told him that I had changed my mind because there was a lot of blame attached to Jaguar, in people's minds, being involved with this big fight with Fangio. I said that I thought we should cancel all the advertising space and he replied that he would phone me back in an hour's time.

'He phoned back and asked if I still felt the same. I said that I did and that all the papers would accept cancellations. So he said, "All right".

'In my opinion, that was about the best decision I ever made.

'Bill Rankin was the Publicity Manager. He was a terribly good fellow and very able. He was the one who had the concept of the Jaguar for the front of the car. We got on famously and I went all over the world with him to all the exhibitions.

'I was the first one to take a Mark VII over to America. I was planning to go and Bill Lyons heard of this and there was a possibility of a dock strike in New York and so he asked me to take it over as my private property. I went on the *Queen Elizabeth* and had a pleasant journey, and they took over the car in New York.

'Bill Rankin certainly played a very large part in creating the Jaguar image. We tried to build an image around Jaguar. We never compared it with other cars, we just built an image around the car, and that was that.

'We came up with the phrase, "A Special Kind Of Motoring". That is different from anybody else, we're not comparing it with anybody. It's just a special kind of motoring, which it was. It was a perfect image of the car.

'Sir William was a great believer in advertising, a very great believer. In fact, during the war, when newspapers were only four-page papers, we had an advertisement every month in the *Daily Mail* and *The Telegraph*. It was just a three-inch double column but that was as much as you could get.

'After the war we adopted the idea of a special size of advertisement which was a quarter of a page across. The publications were loathe to accept it, but it gave you a big image for less money.

'We also gave the name Sovereign to Daimler. Lyons didn't know what to call it and Eric Colbon dreamed it up. But Lyons didn't like long names and he though it was a bit long.

'I said, "It's not because, although it has four syllables, it always sounds like two when you say it". He accepted that, and it was adopted.

'I used to go to all the motor shows around the world, and I was the first advertising man to do this. I well remember the E-type launch at Geneva. It was held in a great park and Eric and I sat in the car that was used for the launch and registered 9600 HP.

'I got in by putting my legs in first, and then my bottom.

'Sir William said, "You don't do it like that, Robert. You put your bottom in first, and then your legs!"'

'We often had to do drawings and paintings of a new model even though we didn't have a photograph because the car wasn't built! We had to take the paintings to him for his comments. Maybe we decided the eventual shape of the car!

———

'Sir William didn't like being projected himself. He was a bit backward about that. That's why, at the XJ6 launch, Bob Berry dreamed up the idea of recording his voice, instead of him having to speak at all the sessions which went on for four days. His image was projected up on the screen, the lights went out and the recording started. It was a good idea.

———

'Sir William was always very proud of his cars, and he alway wanted everybody involved to be very proud of them.

———

Bob Bett and Eric Colbon made a presentation to Sir William Lyons following a long and fruitful business relationship between Jaguar Cars and the Nelson Advertising Agency. (Bob Bett)

These sketches, or flights of fancy, were discovered in Norman Dewis's testing logs. (Norman Dewis)

DR SAMIR KLAT who, whilst doing research at Imperial College, London, developed one of the privately-owned Lightweight E-types to a fascinating degree (as described in the *Jaguar E-Type – The definitive History*) and during a distinguished international business career, held the position of vice-president of the largest General Motors dealership outside the States.

'If it wasn't for William Lyons's sense of shape and eye, Jaguar wouldn't exist today.

'It is style that sells cars. Ninety per cent of people buy a car because it looks good.

'I think the XJ40 is a very nice car, but I do not think it is as far ahead of the opposition as the original XJ was when that came out. When that car came out, I would say it was aesthetically by far the most beautiful saloon car on the road. It is, of course, a question of opinion.

'I still think that 20 years later, though. Its road comfort was far superior to anything else. It had a reasonable performance. But it had two things going horribly against it. The car was about the most unreliable form of transport one could imagine, even from day one. I was in the Lebanon at the time and they sold quite a lot there. It was a powerful car, but they were as unreliable as hell. They had nothing but troubles.

'The other thing was that they had appalling, badly designed small details that would fall off or break, which was a shame. In fact if that car had been produced by the Japanese or the Germans, every six months they would have developed small details. There would have been an evolution.

'My criticism, if I can say it, to the British motor industry generally is that they have *brilliant* ideas on cars. These things are like a child. They arrive, they are born: and then they are left – like the Mini. Today it is exactly the same Mini which Issigonis developed in 1958. It is exactly the same car; but the world has moved.

'The original "Beetlewagon", when it first came out, was an abortion – but every few months it was developed. If you look at a Volkswagen or Porsche manual, every three months you get new bits and pieces. They are constantly upgraded. This they never do here.

———

'Some of the XJ6s, when they went to the Lebanon, had an oil consumption problem. The dealer was having quite an argy-bargy with Jaguar and I suggested that we bored the engines out just slightly, so we had a bit of clearance, on two of the cars. It cured the problem.

'On all the early batches he sold, before they were delivered, he used to whip the head off, send them in, and have them bored slightly oversize. In the absolute sense, they were probably more noisy, but let's look at it in the right perspective. They were noisy, probably for the first half minute, until they warmed up. The other thing is, of the overall noise of an engine, this constitutes, probably, 5-10 per cent of the noise. So if the 5-10 per cent is itself noisier by 5-10 per cent, you are talking about 1 per cent extra noise. Who detects 1 per cent for half a minute?

———

ON WALLY HASSAN:
'There were stories around that Jaguar only bought Coventry Climax to try and get Wally Hassan back. He was probably the only real engine designer they had. I think he was head and shoulders above all those that came after him. You have the evidence. He was the creative brain behind the concept of the XK engine, he was the brains behind all the race winning Coventry Climax engines. Now when a man has so many successful engines, all different types, he must have something. You don't hit it by luck so many times.

'How many other people can be credited with such a successful range of engines?'

The United States preview of the all-new XJ luxury sedan took place in the ballroom of the New York Hilton. (Jaguar Cars US)

Mr Heynes to Sir William Lyons upon the impending retirement of the former. The paper is undated but would be about 1968

DEPARTMENT RE-ORGANISATION
'The question of my retirement and the most suitable successor to the position of Technical Director of the Company is, as we are both aware, a very difficult problem to solve but in the plans which I had in mind, this is completely overshadowed by the question as to how long you yourself intend to remain in control of the Company.

'If you are proposing to be here another three or four years, which I cannot believe, I would offer one solution. If, on the other hand, you intend to retire within the next twelve months, I would certainly be prepared to stay, if you wished, and help in the integration of engineering control in the best possible way, to Jaguar's greatest advantage, in what is apparently going to be the specialist car group.

'This question of the merging of the specialist cars, which I know Sir Donald has agreed will not take place so long as you are in charge, will, I feel, almost certainly be one of his first moves when you relinquish control and I am not at all sure that it will be as bad for the Jaguar name and the Jaguar personnel as it would at first appear. We have a pretty sound group of people here on the engineering side who are quite capable technically of holding their own with the people at the other companies and I think there is little fear of them getting swallowed up into an unidentified amalgam. I feel quite sure that the identity of the cars with their special individualities will be allowed to remain and let us *hope that people have sense to leave the name Jaguar without putting an "L" in front of it, which would certainly ruin our image in America.*

'There is little doubt that if this merging of the specialist cars into a single group takes place, it would be much better for it to take place whilst you were still at the helm and I feel I could be of very considerable assistance in supporting the Jaguar engineering group in such a union, and I feel that you could look after the interests of the employees, particularly the senior staff, very much better than by simply handing over the Company as a going concern.

'Even supposing you were to stay with the Company another two years and the Company was to show an extraordinarily good profit, and the new models did exceptionally well, as I believe they will, this is no guarantee that the three firms in question will not be unified – neither is it any guarantee that when you have gone the best people on the Jaguar staff will be given senior appointments. I believe if the integration took place whilst you were still in the chair, you could lean heavily on the side of the people who have served us so well for so long.

'I would like you to give this matter some thought. Perhaps we could again discuss it when we have our meeting. I am equally anxious, as you are, to do the best I can for the Company which I feel, as you do, is very much a part of me, but a lot must depend on your personal decision on this matter.

'I would assure you that I have not dicussed this matter with anyone else but there is quite a lot of surmise inside and outside the factory as to what is going to happen and the feeling of uncertainty is not assisting the Company to look to the future as it should be doing.

SCHEME ONE

'Assuming that you are remaining with the company a minimum of three to four years, I would not see that there is any point in my staying beyond the launching of the V12 and V8 engines. Someone has to take over some time and this is probably the best time to make arrangements.

'I believe to get satisfactory performance, it would be necessary to have two Technical Directors, who would have to be on the main board, which would be Mr. Knight on the vehicle side and Mr. Hassan on the engine side. We may be faced also with putting someone in charge of styling. I cannot believe that you would want to carry on any longer the styling as it is done today. I think we should start a proper Styling Department run as a unit but with someone in control, so that you could deal with a single man instead of having Mr. Gardner, Mr. Thorp, Mr. Sayer, Mr. Rogers and anyone else who likes to enter into the fray, and by this means we could possibly weld the styling into a single unit. For this job I would recommend Mr. Sayer who I think is the only one wiith originality on the staff, and who has the ability to produce a workable drawing from a model which can be made without a lot of fiddling. His designs are drawn to scale and he talks in the language of the present-day body designer and has a strong engineering background. The only problem is whether his health would stand up to such an appointment, and whether he could adequately control staff.

'Below Director level the split up would be much as I have discussed on many occasions and the suggested family tree is given separately.

SCHEME TWO

'If a merger of the three companies were to take place, I believe there would be strong pressure from the Leyland Group to put in Spencer King, now Technical Director of Triumph, one of the engineers responsible for Rover development in the past, either as Technical Director or Chief Engineering Executive.

'If the merger takes place at an early stage, there is little doubt that the power unit group to handle the specialist car engines could be formed with either Mr. Hassan or Mr. Mundy as Chief Executive. This, I believe, would be most satisfactory from Jaguar point of view. On the chassis side, Mr. Knight's capabilities are well known to Dr. Fogg and to quite a

The chef rose to the occasion and appropriately presented his version of the 'leaper' in ice (Jaguar Cars US)

number of other people in the engineering heirarchy and although it is not quite so certain that we could get him heading the suspension group, I believe we could use considerable influence and with Dr. Fogg's backing I think we could easily be successful.

'On the body side there is little doubt that it is intended that body engineering as such, for all companies, will go to the Pressed Steel Co. and their satellites. This leaves only styling and the decision on models must inevitably remain with the management and the styling department of the individual firms. You would obviously look after this company whilst you were here but it is necessary that someone or some group of people are trained to follow in your footsteps.

'I am afraid this is not quite the direct answer, which I had hoped I would give you, but this matter, which concerns the whole future of the Company, has been so uppermost in my mind, that the positioning of individuals lower down the scale is to me relatively unimportant.'

The feline conductor seems to be having a harsh word with the Jaguar works band. (Jaguar Cars)

From Mr Heynes to Sir William Lyons – 12 August 1968

POINTS FOR DISCUSSION
1) From your note it appears that you are now prepared to give Engineering fuller control of the situation than you have been prepared to do in the past, and I believe, and always have believed, that this is necessary.

Whilst you had your finger completely on the pulse, it operated satisfactorily but such delegation as you have given has not been complete enough to permit the various Directors to operate completely and prove whether they can, or cannot, carry the job.
2) There is no doubt the Company is badly missing Mr. Whittaker who was responsible more than anyone in the organisation for welding the various departments into a single unit. He could, and did, discuss with all the Directors the various day to day problems without any personal aggrandisement, and was virtually the second step in the ladder, which gave cohesion.
3) Mr. Silver as overall Director of the production side, has never been effectively replaced and there is no single man on production who is capable of, or willing to, force through a programme.

Not only were Malcolm Sayer's designs aerodynamically brilliant, but they were so damned beautiful as well. (Jaguar Cars)

One of George Thomson's sketches from his early days in the styling studio. 'This one was done in 1968 when we were doing the XJ27 (XJS). This was the Styling Studio proposal that went up against the one that Malcolm Sayer did and was based on the same package. We did a quarter scale model with Malcolm's one side and on the other side the studio's design, which was mainly Ollie Winterbottom's at the time.'

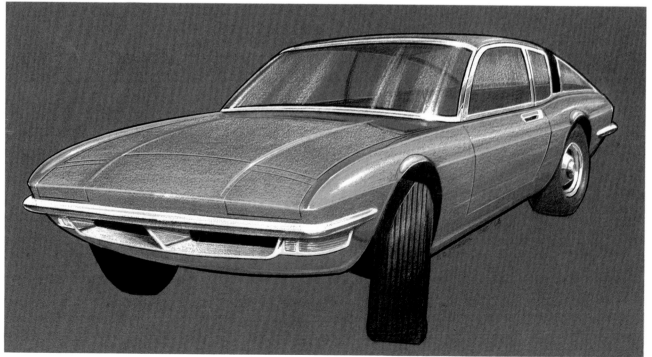

SEVENTIES

AN INTERVIEW WITH BILL HEYNES

'Lyons, although not a trained engineer, knew what he wanted in a car – and more particularly what the public wanted, and he was willing to accept and try any modifications I made.

'At Humber it was a very different state of affairs. After Grinham and Dawtrey, the chief engineers and my immediate bosses, left, new designs were not welcome, unless they came from outside the company. I recall I designed and had made an independent front suspension for the Minx – it was cheap and simple, with an infinitely better ride than the current set-up.

'So the Chief Engineer sent me down to see Col. Cole to explain all about it. He appeared very interested and I thought he appreciated the good points, but then he said, "well Heynes, who else is using this type of design?".

' "No-one else, to my knowledge, sir," I replied. "It's new."

' "Oh well, in that case I think we had better leave it."

'That attitude could never have occurred with Lyons, who was all for innovation, and being new was an immediate attraction to him.

'Lyons was a good chief to work for. He was always approachable and in later years, when we had Board Meetings of a sort, he had become more considerate towards the views of the committee. Although it did not often alter his actions, he perhaps put things in a different way. Perhaps if we on the Board had known of the proposed merger with Austin Morris, we might have talked him out of it – I really don't know. I, for one, would have tried.

'I had already suffered from one merger. That was the Humber/Hillman merger, from which no good came and no better cars were produced.'

JO EERDMANS, former President of Jaguar Cars Inc

Jo Eerdmans is a Dutchman who was working in England during the war. Though his name is not well known, he was to play a very major role in the Jaguar story and was closer to Lyons than, perhaps, anyone else in the Company. He first explained to me how he met Lyons.

'I have got four children and they and my first wife went to Woolacombe in Devon during the Blitz. Lyons had two daughters, and he had a boy, and they were also in Woolacombe and went to the same hotel. I went down every other weekend and he did the same, and so we met. We became friends.

'Later on, in '52, I was Joint Managing Director of the Thomas de La Rue company. We had a big issue on the Board and it was publicised by the newspapers, especially the Daily Express. They wrote that Eerdmans might leave the Board, but I decided to stay and fight it out. I went to see Sir Walter Monkton, who was one of my best friends and Minister of Labour in the Government, and he said to me, "you always wanted to go to America. You have had an offer to start a small company. Don't stay here because you are a Dutchman and with these old Englishmen at de La Rue you will have trouble again."

'So then the *Daily Express* wrote that Jo Eerdmans was going to the United States. Lyons saw it in the paper and 'phoned me immediately. He said, "Can I see you? I'd like you to do something for me in America."

'I said, "OK, I am going to America next week. Can you come to London this week and meet me in the Dorchester Hotel?"

'So he came to the Dorchester in the afternoon and we had tea. He asked me to investigate Jaguar's whole situation in America, and his two distributors, Mr Hornburg and Hoffman. I said, "All right, I can do that, but of course I will carry on with my own little company as well."

'That was OK, and I investigated his market and went to see all the dealers, etc., and found out what was wrong. We then cancelled out Hoffman and Hornburg and we cut down to a small distributor. Then he said to me, "Take over the whole Jaguar business for North and South America, be 100 per cent Jaguar and give up your interest in the other company," which I did, and became 100 per cent a Jaguar man.

'I looked after Jaguar in America and Canada. I started an assembly plant in Mexico City, and sold quite a few in the Carribean. We ran the Mexico plant with Mercedes-Benz. The Mexican Government decided that expensive cars could not be sold for a time, if you brought in the parts. They had to be made in Mexico, which of course was impossible for the small quantity of Jaguars that we sold. So we dropped it and Mercedes went on.

'That is how I met Lyons and joined Jaguar. I went for the first time to the factory and met all his colleagues, and then he came with me to New York. I took an office on Park Avenue, and that is how we started.

'The XK120 had just come in when I went over, and the Mark VII. We didn't sell a lot over here, but gradually I brought it up to about 7,000 cars a year. After the Mark VII shape, we switched over to the "lemon", the Mark X. I should not say the "lemon", but it was not a very good car. It came out at the same time as the Edsel, so there were two "lemons"! So we stopped production and after that came the XJ.

'It took a long time to come out. We had a big distributors' meeting in New York with Lyons, and then in London. We told him what type of a car we wanted, and brought photographs of Buicks and other cars, and told him what we liked on each car. We told him what was the ideal car we would like from Jaguar. So then they designed the XJ6. If they could have done it a little quicker, we would have had a far bigger part of the market.

'The problem with the E-types was that they couldn't make any more. I told Lyons of the possibilities in America and he said he would double the output. It took four or five years before they doubled the output.

'I went over three times a year to Coventry. The organisation in Jaguar was not flexible enough. Lyons, of course, was the owner and he wanted to decide everything. I talked to Heynes, who in my opinion was an outstanding man, and Whittaker was a good man, and we decided what had to be done. Then we went to Lyons and he said he would think it over. It was always, "I'll talk to you next week, I'll talk to you next month".

'Lyons was so conservative in his decisions. He wanted to make certain that everything he was doing was right. I told him that was tripe. "You have got to take your men at the right value, and give them more responsibility. How often do you take all the decisions?"

'He was a dictator.

'I knew that man inside out. His wife knew what he was like as well, and we discussed how to change his outlook on certain things. But you couldn't do it.

JAGUAR ... *always a leap ahead*

On the following two pages are some more of George Thomson's sketches, about which he comments:

'Some of these are more the type of thing that should have happened with the XJ-S, and could have come about at the time. We were trying to get more of a rounded feeling into it, perhaps something more Jaguar-like. We were trying to introduce more softness without necessarily changing some of the aspects that we had on the 'S'.

'The extra plan-form, with more of a nose, and a more rounded tail would have given it, I think, a stronger Jaguar feel — closer to the E-type, without necessarily being an E-type.

'The XJS has the air extractor behind the window panel and that, at the time, was a separate panel and there was no continuity between the two. The glass stopped, then you had body colour and then the extractor. I felt that that area was far too short – it needed a bit of length. It really made the cab look as if it was a small fraction of the car. You'd got all the bonnet, all the back end and this little bit of cab. Unfortunately, the glass proportion wasn't ideal because it's quite shallow inside, but I felt it needed more length.

'I did a series of proposals, (top, page 141) trying to do things with it. Unfortunately, I did one echoing the concave line which was picked as the way to go. Really I didn't feel happy

with it at the time. I would have gone away from the concave line and gone for something like one of the lower two to try and disguise it a bit!

  'I did some detail work on the later E-types. We looked at a lot of different knaves with various sections – flush, recessed and proud. We were picking up ideas from the Mark II/240/340 saloons and so on.'

'When he became "Sir" William Lyons everything changed. Before that he always gave a Christmas party for his top executives at his beautiful home. As soon as he became Sir William, nobody was ever invited again, not even Heynes or Whittaker for a meal or a drink.

  'When I came into the picture as an old friend, every time I came over, he would say that I must go for dinner one evening, so I always did. That upset the other Directors, especially Lofty England. Heynes understood. I could talk to him and Whittaker. But Lofty is more aggressive and he didn't like it.

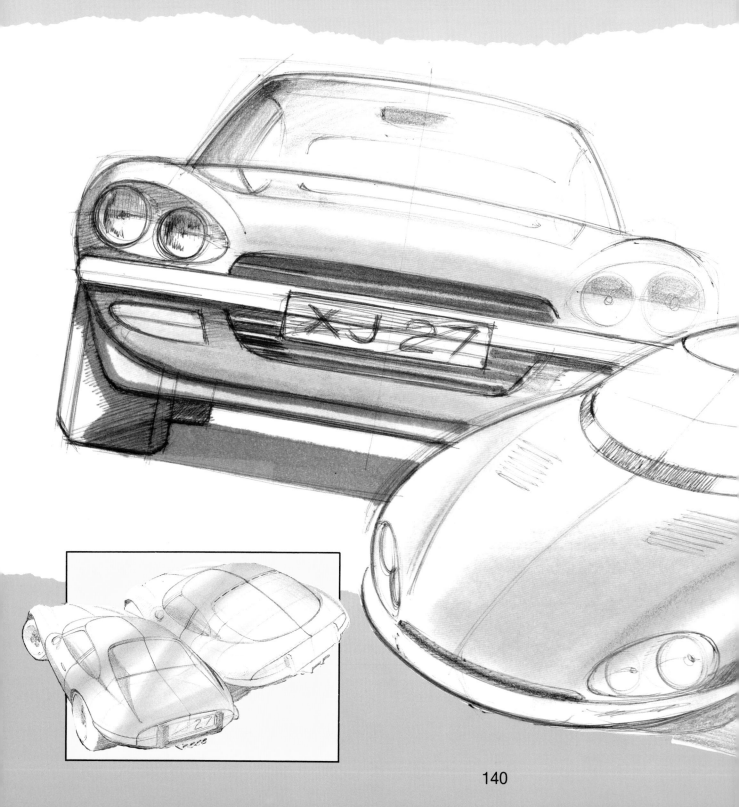

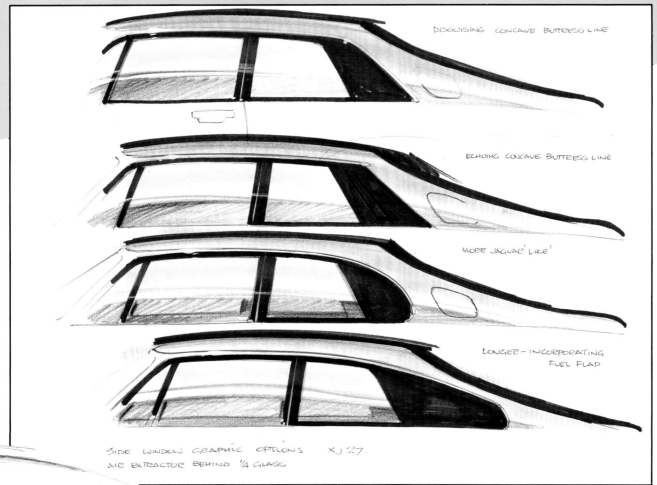

DISGUISING CONCAVE BUTTRESS LINE

ECHOING CONCAVE BUTTRESS LINE

MORE 'JAGUAR' LIKE'

LONGER - INCORPORATING FUEL FLAP.

SIDE WINDOW GRAPHIC OPTIONS   XJ 27.
AIR EXTRACTOR BEHIND ¼ GLASS

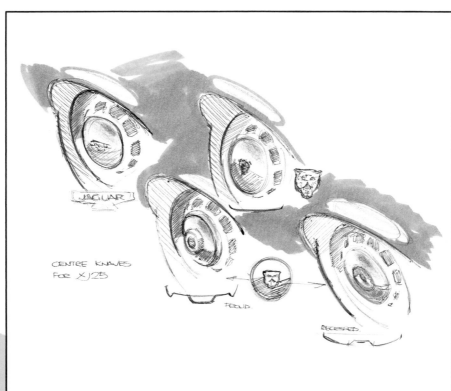

JAGUAR

CENTRE KNAVES
FOR XJ25

PROUD.

RECESSED

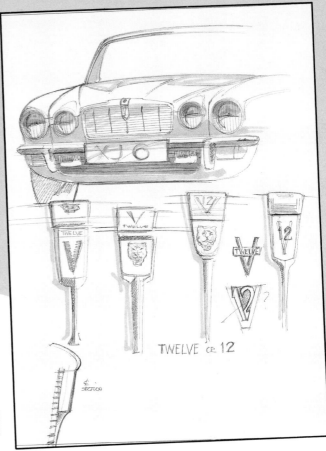

George Thomson: 'I was involved in bringing the Series I XJ saloons up to Series II, and here we were looking at what we could do. We knew that we had to lift the bumper to meet the American regs and it was a question of whether we brought the bumper up completely, or whether you brought it up, but had overriders instead of taking it right across, allowing you to keep a more traditional grille.

'I spent a fair bit of time looking at badging for the new Series II XJ grille, as to how we could blend it into the new front. We spent a lot of time on detail like that.'

Right: *This is why Jaguar bought Daimler. They needed the space at the Radford plant! (Jaguar Cars)*

'It was wrong too. I told Lyons he was wrong and that he must invite the others too. But my relationship was very, very pleasant with him, and with Heynes and Whittaker. The financial man, Huckvale, and I really became friends, because Huckvale saw in me a man who might change things, but I couldn't make many changes.

I asked Jo Eerdmans if he was his own boss in the States.

'Nobody ever interfered with me. I saw Lyons when he came over perhaps every two years. I made a profit every year and I just showed him the accounts so that he could see how much money we had made, and he was happy. I always told him we could do more.

'I had a very happy relationship, as I say, with Heynes and Whittaker, and really with Lofty as well. Lofty was really a good fellow, but he was so sarcastic.

'When Lyons's son was killed, slowly Lyons said to me, "I must appoint somebody who can take my place when I have an accident or when I am gone". So we talked about this for a long time, and I gave him advice, saying. "Don't bring in a new man. You will upset the present Directors, etc., etc. Take Lofty." I was really the man who proposed Lofty to get the big job over there.

'Lyons said, "I'm amazed at you because I thought you were big enemies".

'I replied, "We are not big enemies, but we are arguing all the time because he's sarcastic, and then I can be sarcastic too. So we tease each other all the time. But I think if you train him and you put him next door to you in an office, and see him for half an hour every day, and tell him what you think, the way he should do it and the way he should not do it, and the way he did it yesterday was wrong, then he can become a very good man." And that is what happened.'

During his long and immensely distinguished career, Eerdmans was made a CBE and had dealings with many famous politicians.

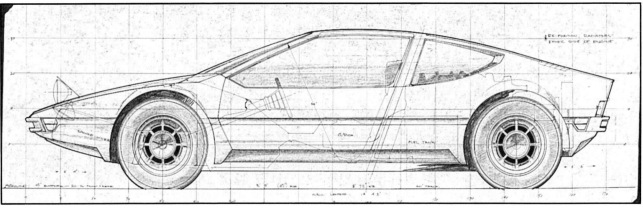

George Thomson comments on the above sketches: 'This was really an attempt at altering the back end of the XJS in '72 to try to take away the concave shape that was in the rear sails. I don't think anybody was really happy with the XJS rear end but it was a bit of a tricky area to deal with. We had got away from the big glass hatch like the E-type, which had a hatch that was more glass than sheet metal. There was definitely some Ferrari Dino influence.
'I think at the time they were too far down the road with the sheet metal tooling. We were really trying to keep, say, from the door forward as it was, but then rearwards reduce the twist

'Macmillan was great. I admired that man so much. I talked to him quite a bit. When he came to the New York Show in 1962, I said to him, ' "Just come up to the Jaguar office for a little while and have a glass of Champagne".

"Oh, no, no," he said, "no Champagne. If you can get me a good old Bourbon, then I come up. We got hold of some Bourbon and so we had two or three. He was very human.

'I knew Gaitskill since he was 30 years old. He came over to New York and we had a meeting with him at the Consul's home. I was then President of the Chamber of Commerce so I was in charge of the meeting. He comes in, looks at me and says, "Mr Eerdmans how are you?" I hadn't seen him for years, but he apologised for not wearing the cufflinks that I had given him when I was with de La Rue!

'When there was the big battle about Stokes, I wrote to Harold Wilson and said, "Don't support Stokes. I have known Stokes for years and years. He is a first class salesman, but he is not an administrator. He won't be able to do it."

'That was the downfall of the whole set-up. I never got an answer to that letter. I wrote to him before about the situation in America and I got a letter back of 10 pages from Wilson. But when I wrote to him about Stokes – no answer!

'I sat in a Board Meeting when the deal was really made by Sir George Harriman and Sir William Lyons. Sir George Harriman, of course, didn't know anything about the business at all, about the financial side in any case. They came to an agreement in principle. So it was worked out by Ron Lucas and a few other fellows. Ron was really helping as the Vice Chairman then. I went to the next meeting and discussed all the details. Then there was another meeting a few days later, and Ron Lucas got up and said, "don't forget Sir William, we did not merge with Jaguar. We bought Jaguar. You are just part and parcel of us, and of course the bosses are the bosses of BMC."

'Then Lucas said, "we want a BMC man to run the business in America". I was 63, with two years to go before I could retire. I had an agreement with Lyons that I had a pension here in America, that he would remain a member of the Board, that his son would carry on the business, he would remain on the Board in England till he died, and I could remain on the Board in America until I died, and would have $---- a month for my position here.

'So I proposed that Graham Whitehead become my successor and take over the whole caboodle in America, as I knew him very well and I thought he could do a damn good job. I said I would help him all I could and that was accepted. I said this was on one condition, that I could remain on the Board, as I had agreed with Lyons, and have my fee. Lucas and the others said this was OK and I asked them to put it in the minutes.

'They went broke within a year and Stokes came in. I talked to Stokes about the arrangement. I said to Lyons, "We've got to settle this". He went six times to Stokes to talk about my arrangement with Jaguar. Stokes never gave a proper answer to Lyons and Lyons phoned me up at home one day, and said, "Look I'm not going to see that man anymore. He drives me crazy."

'Sir William never wanted to put anything in writing. We were old friends and I trusted him completely. But when the company was taken over, things changed. It was a drama!

'The very funny thing is that when Sir William Lyons made an agreement with BMC, I had just worked out an agreement with Daf in Holland, to go together with them. They would make the small cars and Jaguar the luxury cars, and sell the cars all over the world, the trucks and everything. Now look at DAF, it is a terrific success. And we went down like anything. Now we are up again, thank God.'

When I mentioned to Jo that Leyland Trucks and DAF had just merged, he could only laugh ruefully.

———————

'LEYLAND CARS – A CALL FOR SANITY, BUT TOO LATE?' by a Jaguar employee

'I am writing this open letter to those who care about what is currently happening to Leyland Cars in the hope that something can be salvaged from this rapidly sinking company. This is my cry to register the common feelings of those who can see the universal demoralisation that is going on around them, amongst those who can't or won't.

'Most of us have stood and watched the reorganisation and the tragic results of over-centralisation become more and more evident as each day passes. All those who directly affect the product of the company, the engineers throughout each individual factory and the men and women who build the motor cars, share the same views about our

that was coming across the rear. This was an attempt to do something with the vehicle as it stood.

'This [immediately above] is an original drawing I did in 1969/70. There was a proposal to have an arc of 34 inches struck from the 'H' (hip) point and you had to keep the windscreen clear of that, which meant that you had a tremendous distance between the head and the windscreen header.

'I looked at a proposal using a V12 engine, turned round 'à la Countach' with the gearbox between the seats. The fuel tanks were either side of the engine and I put the radiator at the back but with the possibility of also positioning the radiators at either side of the engine (like today's Testarossa). It had 4-inch deep bumpers set at 16 to 20 inches to comply with the American regs.

'The starting point, though, was the proposed 34 inch regulation and it is funny how one single regulation can lead on to something.

'A lot of things I did at my time at Jaguar, like this one, were not official. It was a case of "well, what can I do next? Nobody's pushing me to do anything for work. I'll see what I can do."

'It was looked at and I did a colour rendering of it, and had it up in the studio for a long while. It's hard to remember if anybody made any comments. I think about the only comments that we did get was that the engine looked like an upside down pig – a sow that is!'

These illustrations were done in the Styling Department in 1973 with thoughts of the XJ6 replacement in mind.

future; the once very evident pride which enabled the great companies Jaguar, Rover and Triumph to produce world-beating motor cars has been so terribly shattered by the irrational policy to abolish autonomy. The situation is now so totally out of hand that sensible, thinking people cannot allow themselves to really care any longer, so there are growing signs of abandonment and surrender to the idea that maybe we'll muddle through.

'Nobody really believes that we are going about things the right way but it just seems easier for the moment if we pretend we might be.

'The reasons behind this apparently ludicrous reorganisation are difficult to recognise from the point of view of each individual company, but when looking from the viewpoint of a central committee one can more easily imagine why this was instigated. When Lord Ryder was given the task of appraising the position and deciding upon the correct course of action for British Leyland, he surveyed each plant and saw how massive and diversified the various companies were and realised that no one committee could control all these as they stood. The logical action from his point of view was to combine everything as far as possible into several manageable divisions, namely:- Sales and Marketing, Customer Service Operations and Manufacturing and Assembly.

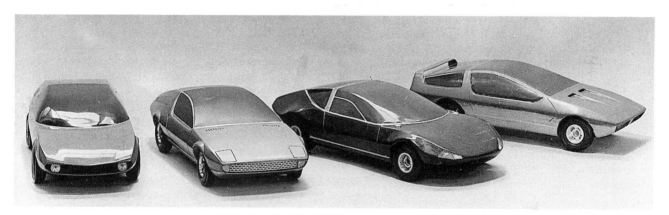

'This, Lord Ryder believes, would afford the National Enterprise Board blanket control over each operation, would reduce the overall head count necessary to run them and therefore be more efficient. The intention was to avoid each company having to do its own manufacturing, assembly, marketing and servicing independently, hence utilising four or more complete sets of staff, one for each company and centralise them all so that one Leyland Cars corporate image could be formed and projected throughout.

'In many other industries this would have worked and it showed that Lord Ryder was basically a sound businessman, but unfortunately it exposed his complete ignorance of the delicacies of the motor industry. The NEB of course had no experience of the internals of the motor business to know any wiser so the committee jointly agreed upon this seemingly grand idea.

'When the plans were announced there was much internal mumbling throughout all the factories about why they simply wouldn't work but nobody of any importance shouted loudly enough to make the NEB understand that there was no way their plans could work. Those who did attempt to register their justified protests were discouraged when their energy appeared to be wasted on deaf ears.

'Soon there was to be the Earls Court Motor Show of 1975 and for the first time the public would see Jaguars, Austins, Triumphs, Morris' and MGs all displayed side by side under the big Leyland Cars banner. Most people recognised how ridiculous it was for different companies with different histories and totally different aims to present themselves together as one fraternity but unfortunately the NEB and the

These four models were created by George Thomson and Chris Greville-Smith in the Styling Department, and were entered for an annual competition organised by Vauxhall. (Jaguar Cars)

147

brainwashed Board of Directors were still patting each other on the back and drinking gin and tonics to celebrate the splendid co-operation.

'Since then we have watched one after another moral stronghold compounded into wretched centralisation. Sales and marketing functions disappeared from each of the factories to combine under two roofs at Longbridge and Redditch. Service operations for Jaguar, Rover and Triumph were temporarily centralised at Allesley but with the intention of having all the actual servicing carried out at one centre in Bickenhill.

'During these impending moves the people at Jaguar fought harder than most of the others, understandably because they had by far the most to loose as a result of centralisation. Fortunately for Jaguars and their customers, enough strong minded members of the workforce maintained their views that Jaguar customers could not be adequately looked after by Austin/Morris or Rover/Triumph staff and the Kingfield Road Jaguar/Daimler Service Department remained to provide workshop facilities operated by specialised and qualified staff for Jaguar owners whose problems their dealers were unable to resolve.

'But factories of Jaguar, Rover and Triumph soon lost their names to become known as just Leyland Plants. This massacre even extended to the discontinuance of the name Jaguar on letterheadings, compliments slips, factory gates, internal publications and, many feared, the product itself. The effect of this anti-marque policy was felt immediately by all those within the factories. Men and women whose life was devoted to creating a fine product and hence a reputation for their companies with pride, enthusiasm and trust were suddenly deprived of their identity, their aims and their ambitions and were expected by an unknown group of men somewhere in London to work towards a doubtful goal under a meaningless name of Leyland whch had no history and, in their minds, certainly no future.

'Distrust and bad feelings crept quickly throughout each plant and the lowering in morale of the workforce soon became apparent in the quality of the product which steadily worsened in proportion to the amount of interference they were being subjected to. The entire workforce knew what was going wrong and many trusted that surely the management would also see where their mistakes were and correct their policy before it was too late. But "the management" were remote from the plants and remained blind to what was happening. The NEB instructed the Directors to plough blindly on and keep centralising until nobody would remember their names.

'It appears that now the Board of Directors is so committed to the original plans of Lord Ryder, many feel there is no backing out, even though Lord Ryder himself backed out by resigning. The tragedy is that his underlings trusted him so totally that they have continued to cling regardlessly to his original plan, despite the very apparent disastrous consequences.

'The current signs of our direction are shown by widespread customer dissatisfaction, very poor workmanship, poor total volume performance, continually worsening industrial relations, extraordinarily high staff turnover particularly at senior levels, and general public bitterness towards the British Motor Industry.

'Most of us know the proper answer. Give each factory its autonomy and thereby restore employees' faith in "their" company and pride in "their" work. Motor cars are emotive products and the people who produce them are naturally emotional about their creations. Leyland Cars is far too huge for any one man to govern and too massive for any employee to feel part of. This is a case where in the high handed business atmosphere of the Board of Directors conference room, the feelings, opinions and importance of the people who ultimately make the product have been entirely neglected. Job satisfaction for many disappeared when the identities of the companies were deliberately eroded. Since then the workforce have demanded augmented financial reward to replace the

previous psychological reward of producing a fine product and putting "your" name on it.

'Are we going to continue running our companies into the ground and rely increasingly upon taxpayers to merely delay the final crunch which cannot now be very far away? The result of Leyland Cars collapsing will not only entail massive unemployment throughout the country, but will also lead to the most tragic and far reaching economic recession since the war.

'The facts are painfully undisguised, the evidence is conspicuous and now the choice is ours. To quote Lord Ryder, albeit out of context: "I do not doubt for one moment that British Leyland can be strong and viable – provided the will is there. But there is not a moment to lose."

'The damage is being done now, soon it will be too late, let us take a turn for the better.'

CRAIG JENKINS
Ex-apprentice, Jaguar Cars Ltd

ENGINE WEIGHTS AS INSTALLED ON TESTBED FOR PERFORMANCE TESTS

Less fan, air pipes, and air cleaner, clutch, clutch housing and gearbox.

With exhaust manifolds, flywheel and all electrical equipment. All weights with engine dry.

Type	Weight in lbs	Remarks
240	503$\frac{1}{2}$	
280	538$\frac{1}{2}$	Engine not built; main details as 3-litre
280 HERON	516$\frac{1}{2}$	As above – V12 Heron head substituted for XK
3 LITRE	538$\frac{1}{2}$	
340	567	
380	592	
420	605	
XJ6 V8 3.6	504	
XJ6 V12 5.3	612	
DAIMLER V8 XDM	437$\frac{1}{2}$	
DAIMLER V8 DQ.450	612	

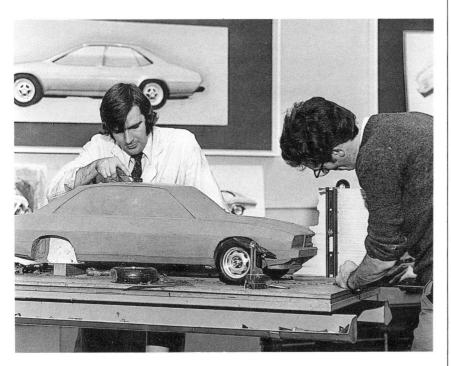

A couple of Jaguar stylists work on a model whilst grappling with the problem of succeeding the Lyons XJ6. (Jaguar Cars)

This Californian XJ saloon, seen leaving De Monte Forest, has the registration VYKS CAT, which is presumably a reference to the owner, but the significance of the photo is that it was taken from the seat of no less a machine than a Bugatti Royale (by my old chum, Nick Baldwin).

HARRY ROGERS joined in 1937 and retired in 1973. He worked particularly closely with Lyons

'I served my time as a coachbuilder at Cross and Ellis's where I graduated from being an apprentice to a gang leader. I stayed there a few years and then I went to Charlesworth Bodies, in Coventry. They used to do work for Daimler and Alvis, but then they went on short-time. We were only working nine till four, and no Saturdays. Of course in those days we used to do 47 hours a week.

'So in between eight and nine, I went up to S.S Cars and obtained a promise of a job there. That was 1937 and I was 29.

'It was a terrible place really. I'd been used to wearing a white apron as a woodworker, building these beautiful motor cars which then went to the panel beaters to be panelled. We always used English ash on the body.

'S.S. were in the old White and Poppe shell filling factory at Holbrook, and it was built on stilts. It was terrible really. They were using tons of lead to fill the body seams up. The fumes were dreadful. I used to come home in the evening and my teeth were all black from the solder.

'But I soon got known, as I'd come from Charlesworths, and they were having quite a bit of trouble producing the motor car on the finishing end of it. Somebody had told Bill Lyons that I had been all through it, and he came up to me on the track one day and he says, "I've been told that you worked at Charlesworth Bodies. Have you ever fitted any Sharvester [?] locks?"

'I said, "Of course I have, yes".

' "We're having a dickens of a job, we can't get the doors to shut."

'They were all rubber mounted, dove-tailed and what-have-you.

'I said, "The secret of that is to have a perfect line-up from your hinges".

'He then asked me to go round the end of the track and get as many doors sorted as possible. He told the boss on the line what I was doing. All I had was a pencil, and I drew the strike line and that's where the striker went. And every one shut first time.

'He came down at the end of the day and said, "Oh, you're getting on well". We'd got the output out that day, which was 28 cars a day. I mentioned that I didn't want to be on it too long because the way I was going, I would never work back because the track was going at about the same speed as I was clearing the locks. So he said he would get me a couple of people to help, and I taught them.

'Then I got back on my own job, which was door hanging in, what they called, the bodyshop. It was terrible! I'd never been used to that sort of thing. It was an all-steel job, and you worked one side, whilst your mate worked the other side, on these two doors. Then there was another man who used to do the bootlids, and hang the little spare wheel lids on the bottom. We used to have a welder as well. When you first hung the doors on, ooh, they was all dropping everywhere. So you got a lever and he warmed all round the wheel-arch, what we called the "D" post, and he used to get that all red hot. You'd take the big lever, and a big hammer, 'cause we all had about a four pound hammer, and "bump" on to the wheel-arch. The door would shoot up!

'That wasn't my cup of tea at all. To cut a long story short, by '38 I'd had enough, and I was trying to get into the Experimental Shop. But a chap named Wicketts, who was the Foreman of the Body Shop, wouldn't let me go. He wouldn't hear of it.

'Any road Chamberlain went over to see Hitler and came back with a paper, "Peace in our Time". That was the signal to start on aircraft, so then I was directed down to the Experimental. My mate had to stay and finish the sanction of bodies – do both sides – then eventually he came down. That was when the war started.

John Barber, a senior Director of British Leyland, once asked Sir William Lyons what he thought was the maximum number of cars that Jaguar could sell annually. The answer was 37,000.

'We had a new building built up at the top, and we started on the Short Stirling wings – leading edges and trailing edges. I was allocated to the leading edge, and I was fitting all the pipework. On the leading edge there was so many hooks, and that was to catch hold of the barrage balloons. When they were triggered, a shot was fired which went through the cable. That was the idea!

'I had to join either the fire brigade, Home Guard or first aid, so I picked the fire brigade. I was on every eighth night – I did a night on and then worked again next day. I got to leading fireman and had a crew. Even the bosses joined in and we used to have to train Whittaker and Lyons to put incendiary bombs out, and that sort of thing.

'Where we scored over the Home Guard – they used to have to march in church parades, and goodness-knows-what, and we just had night duties. We then went on to the Lancaster bomb doors. There was three of us allocated on to that job, and I was in charge of it. Some loom factory up north sent all the iron work on concrete bases for the assembly. It was all part of a loom, I suppose, or something to do with weaving. We had to alter it and add pieces, to assemble these bomb doors.

'The bomb door was 34 foot long, 4 foot 6 inches one end and tapered down to about four foot the other. There were seven hinges and inner and outer skins, and you had to be really accurate. There were 22,000 rivets in each one and every one was examined.

'Then we took over the Gloster Meteor from Standard. They'd had it for two years, and could only produce one a week, or something! When we got cracking on that, we were producing five.

'After the war, we went down the cellars and got out all the pre-war bodies and bits and pieces, and started again. We got back into production with these cars.

'Lyons was very close with me. I think he trusted me, and I never dared tell him a lie. I was always honest with the chap. He used to come in when I was running the Shop, and he'd always wheedle a date out of me for the completion of something.

'Then he would come in and say, "It's getting very close, Rogers".

'Once I told him I hadn't got the modified drawing and he asked who was supposed to give me those. I replied that it was Mr Baily.

Jimmy Stewart drove for Ecurie Ecosse in 1953/54 and the factory team in 1955 before retiring. He is seen standing beside XKD 501 which he drove at Silverstone and the Nürburgring during his 'factory' year. On his left is his up-and-coming young brother, Jackie, who would achieve a little success in the same field. The car on the right is a Tojeiro. (Jackie Stewart)

' "Well, go and tell him you want them now.

'Of course Mr Baily had got a posh job. I told him I'd come from Mr Lyons and it was getting close to the date when I'd promised this job, and he's sent me for the drawing.

"Ooh," he said, "that's impossible."

'I said, "I can't go back and tell him that".

'He says, "You'll have to. It's impossible. We haven't got them."

'I went back and saw Lyons and told him that it was impossible.

' "Oh," he said, "it's no good sending you, I can see." So he went himself. I felt very small! But he came back with the drawings. All the figures were altered in pencil. He asked if I could work with them and I said that of course I could.

' "Get on with it then." That was typical! That was Bill Lyons!' recalls Harry with great amusement and obvious fondness for the man. 'If he wanted something he was the boss and he could get it.

'Another instance proved that. Mr Heynes was always trying to make a big job out of things, and that's why changing a model took three or four years. But Lyons was the boss, and he wanted to change in 12 months. They'd come in and we'd almost got the car finished and Heynes would say, "All this chrome here, it'll all reflect in the window at night".

'And old Lyons said, "Well we'll give them a tin of black paint and a brush". And that was it. It went through. That was typical Bill Lyons.

'The first body that we didn't have much to do with was the Mark VII. But while the Body Drawing Office and Pressed Steel were getting on with the Mark VII, we produced the Mark V, which was a stage up from the pre-war models.

'I drew all that. I did all the drawing full size on plywood boards, and I was working for a chap named Robinson at the time. He was a marvellous chap for ideas, and I used to carry them out for him.

'Bill Robinson was frightened to death that someone would come along and cut up one of these boards wanting some plywood. So it was decided that we would employ a junior draughtsman allocated to our Shop, which was called the Experimental Development Department. That junior draughtsman turned out to be Cyril Crouch.

'He took all my boards and produced it on paper, and it was all filed in the library. When that was done, we'd finished with Cyril Crouch – we'd got no use for him. So we went to Bill Thornton, who was the Chief Draughtsman at the time, and told him we'd got a good chap – could he make use of him?

' "Ooh no," he says, "I've got enough." He'd got three draughtsmen! Any road, we wouldn't be put off and we went to Heynes, and Bill Heynes made him have him. In no time at all, Cyril was running the Drawing Office, and he eventually took over from Bill Thornton, when Bill Thornton retired.

'Abbey Panels made most of the panels for the racing cars to the formers that I made. We assembled them when they came back. We had a specialist welder in because it wasn't just aluminium, it was aircraft material.

'We used to have the drivers come in to be fitted: Mike Hawthorn, Duncan Hamilton, Tony Rolt – who was very tall and wanted a bit more legroom – Peter Walker and, in the early days, Stirling Moss. I think it was Mike Hawthorn who had a soft spot in Lyon's heart. Lyons was knocked about when Hawthorn was killed.

After Harry had been ill, Lyons arranged for Mr and Mrs Rogers to go to Geneva for the E-type launch and they bumped into Sir William at Heathrow. The Rogers had been booked on an earlier flight but had been given the wrong tickets.

'He knew my wife had got butterflies in her stomach about flying.

"Ooh," he said, "you don't want to worry. That plane you were going on was only a twin-engined thing. I wouldn't travel with anything under four engines."

'He let us go first up the steps. Somebody called out to him when we got on but he came and sat by us. When they started bringing the lunches round, he said he'd better go and have lunch with these people otherwise they might think it funny if he ignored them. But he said he would be back. I thought, "That's the last we shall see of him".

'He didn't like me smoking. He was always telling me it was no good for me, and he didn't drink as such. He'd drink a sherry, with an egg in it, or something like that, for his breakfast. I'd gathered all this from his chauffeur.

'Anyway he did, he came back. There I was with me glass of beer and a fag on. I felt blinking awful. Then the stewardess came round with this tray. Without looking up, I said, "No thank you". I thought it was cigarettes.

"She wants your money for your beer," said Lyons. Oh, dear! So I put my hand in my pocket. Going away, I'd got everything in my pocket. I'd got a bit of string, a pocket knife, but I'd got no change. It was only a shilling.

'He said, "I only had a fruit juice, dear. Mine's free."

OLIVER WINTERBOTTOM, formerly a Jaguar apprentice, was an early member of the Styling Department set up in the late sixties, before moving to Lotus, on to TVR and back to Lotus Cars

'I wanted to be a Jaguar apprentice and went for the interview in the first week of March 1961. It was a week or two before the E-type was to be announced, and factory tours had been stopped for that reason. But under the circumstances, I was taken on a factory tour.

'Halfway through the plant were these amazing vehicles. The impact at the time was unbelievable.

'I stood there, and of course it was like a D-type, and I sort of said, "What the hell are these?".

'The chap replied, "You are not supposed to see, but within a week it'll be out at the Geneva Show. It's our new sports cars."

'And I just said, "I don't believe it!"

'I joined Jaguar in September of that year and started a five year automobile engineer apprenticeship.

'Then later on the XJ-S came along and there were all sorts of internal struggles as to whether it ought to be a replacement E-type or not.

'I did a body for the XJ-S which was a sort of successor to the ideas on the E-type. Looking at a photograph of it now, it wasn't really as good as the E-type idea. It had a cab that was vaguely reminiscent of the Rapier of the day, to give a fastback, and was probably a bit too stylish rather than the pure functional form. It wasn't strange, which you could say the XJ-S was!

'Of course, the XJ-S was never really a replacement for the E-type, and whether that was the right or the wrong thing, I suppose we'll never know. It may have been held back by the fact that it was always based on the XJ6 floorpan, with a shortened wheelbase.

'I have a theory that as people get older – when management in general gets older – the products start to appeal to an older and older man.

'You don't get 20-year-old people designing stuff for 60-year-old men, and you don't get 60-year-old people designing stuff for 20-year-old people. So companies go through cycles and one of the difficulties is when you get to the 60-year-old bit, and all the old guard retire.'

The Jaguar company produced a special envelope to complement the 50th anniversary celebrations in 1972. (Philip Porter)

SWALLOW TO JAGUAR 1922-72

H.W. Porter, Esq.,

Managing Director

Harolds Gauges Limited

Frederick Street

Birmingham B1 3HS

Oliver Winterbottom was, as noted, an early member of the small Styling Department created in the late sixties.

'Bill Thornton and those sort of people gave up their area of responsibilities reluctantly. Fred Gardner did particularly. As far as he was concerned, he was "the bloody Old Man's man, and sod the rest of you"!

'He actually physically frightened you – well, he did me, as an apprentice. He would throw you out of his workshop, and he wouldn't even stop to get your explanation as to why you were there. If you weren't supposed to be there as far as he was concerned, you got out.

'Lyons I saw quite a lot of and I always liked him a lot. There was great respect and we all quaked, because he was the big boss. He was an awfully nice man – he was a gentleman, and there aren't too many of those about.

'He got to know who I was and when I left the company, he actually called me up to his office and asked me why I was going. I said, "I've been here for 10 years now. I'm not going to make much more progress, whereas going to Lotus will be a tremendous opportunity, broaden my experience and, perhaps, one day I could come back to Jaguar".

'He said, "I think you're absolutely right".

'I was very flattered.

'Then as soon as I left, he left! Well, he obviously gave up when he saw I'd gone! I left in December '71 and he went at the end of the January or February following.

'He used to do these so-called drawings if he was trying to explain that a line on a model, or whatever, wasn't quite what he wanted. He used to get the pen and he couldn't draw a normal line – it was always little wispy strokes, so the whole thing looked like a groundhog, or something, when he'd finished it. You can imagine an XK120, which by the time it was finished actually looked as if it was made of nylon fur! He didn't have that one-stroke purpose that you'd expect him to have.

'What he really was, was an incredible judge of good taste.

'I saw quite a lot of Malcolm Sayer on a project that Mike Kimberley and I were involved in, which had the 2¹/₂-litre Daimler V8 engine, front-mounted, and beam axle rear suspension on a car based on the Alfa Sprint dimensions but, I think, with four inches in the wheelbase. It was seen as a replacement for the Mark II. We just put together a clay model and some drawings, and that was where I first met Mike Kimberley in any sort of depth. He worked upstairs in Malcolm's private office area.

'I remember the headlights were higher than the top of the nose. It had a fastish sort of back, with a separate boot – it was not a hatchback or anything like that. Although the proportions were different, there was an awful lot of similarity in the ideas with the TR6. We weren't allowed pop-up headlights. They were pretty unusual. The Elan had them by then but not many cars did and they were considered to be expensive and complex and heavy.

'Stuck with the 24-inch headlamp height requirement, not wanting twin headlamps because, again, that was expensive and everything was very price conscious, we had a big seven-inch headlamp and therefore the tops of them stuck up above the nose.

'I actually borrowed an Alfa from a friend of mine. England was very keen on this and Lyons was taking quite an interest in it. We decided that the rear seats were too small, because it was a GT, but four inches should do us as a close-coupled saloon.

'We had the Daimler engine, which was nice and short instead of the big old six- cylinder, which was going to dictate the car. The front end was probably twin wishbone – I don't know – it wasn't anything revolutionary. It was all kept pretty compact and wasn't too wide.

'We got very excited about it but the project only lasted about two and a half months, and we collided with the start of British Motor Holdings, and there were all sorts of vehicles looming up on the horizon that this thing might collide with. Then shortly after Triumph and Rover came along and it just got dropped.

'Also, and we didn't realise it at the time, Jaguar were having an awful job to pay for the XJ6.

'Mike Kimberley's role was to guide us on the mechanical packaging aspects, because we were supposed to be stylists and nothing else. There was nothing done on how the body was pressed, or anything like that. It was obviously going to be steel and the bright bits were going to be chrome, although we wondered whether stainless steel could be whispered, as rather more up to date!

'The interior, which was never designed, was obviously going to be wood and leather, but with that rather crafty combination of artificial materials mixed in to make the thing cost right.

'Today it would have been relatively fashionable because it had a high tail. The back end was definitely higher than the front. It had a highish kick-up to the boot, a little like an Avenger, and was probably, in its day, a little bit ahead of its time. The front end, though, might have tired a bit quickly. It did not have, as I recall, a traditional Jaguar grille. I think we just had a horizontal opening, or it may have just had a general ring of chrome in a very wide shape.

'I know we were conscious of the problems we were getting into with grille shapes, although luckily Jaguar had kept moving with the times in terms of air intakes. There were certain shapes that were trade

TONY LOADES, Managing Director of ABBEY PANELS, who supplied E-type bonnets and other major panels
'We were given one week's notice of production finishing. The car could still have been running today, because the tools would have lasted forever.'

ON THE XJ-S CABRIOLET
'Other firms claim to have built the Cabriolet prototypes. We did five here – all different. None of them were drawn. Jim Randle walked in here and said, "We'll do it this way". We did convertibles, targas – indeed, I had a Porsche at the time and we took the roof off my Porsche Targa and we X-rayed it, because you can't get a Targa roof as a spare. They won't sell them, unless you show them your old ripped one. It must have cost Porsche a lot to design that collapsible targa roof. So we X-rayed it to see if we could make use of it, but in fact they used a central bar instead.

'We built it with a central bar, we built it without a central bar, and we built it without anything at all, just the windscreen.'

TONY LOADES

marks and obvious links. The vertical elipse of the XK120/140/150 got sort of turned on its side for the E-type. That broke the mould and enabled you to start the line again. Of course the Mark VII had got squashed down through the Mark X and then subsequently into the XJ range. You could lean those backwards, forwards, anything else, unlike poor old Rolls-Royce, who got completely stuck with only really being able to change the height of the thing.

'I have a feeling that, at that stage, if we had anything, it was just a vague outline. I am sure we had the typical raised bonnet section, which stopped it looking quite as much like a TR6 and rather more like a Jaguar.

'The side was sort of broken dihedral of the day. It was only a two-door – we didn't try for the rear door.

'It could have been a smashing car.

Wolf Nasdala's 120 Drophead Coupé rests in a typically Mediterranean setting, at Cannes to be precise, in 1978. (Wolf Nasdala)

'The other thing that was interesting was the rebodied SP250 Daimler. I don't know who actually did the body but a very nice looking car was built in glass-fibre, and it looked very distantly like a Sunbeam Alpine. In other words, it had a fairly simple opening at the front with a pair of high-mounted headlamps, exposed, a more-or-less straight-through wing line with a vestige of fins at the rear, and therefore vertical rear lamps, a lower set deck lid in between, and a fairly simple wrap-around windscreen.

'There were a couple of prototypes and I remember one which was a dark maroon colour which was stored for a long time almost in the roof of the bus assembly part of the Radford plant along with a couple of the Royal Daimlers and things. It got sold to a guy in Lutterworth – strange we even sold it to anybody.

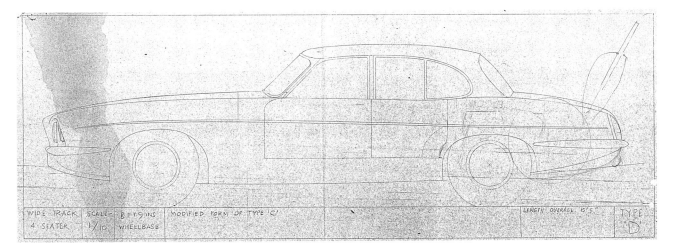

WIDE TRACK | SCALE | 8 FT 9 INS | MODIFIED FORM OF TYPE 'C' | | LENGTH OVERALL 15'5" | TYPE
4-SEATER | 1/10 | WHEELBASE | | | | 'D'

'It had an E-type interior squeezed into it and it had some extra bracing in the chassis, which wouldn't have been difficult, and it had rack and pinion steering, probably based on the E-type, and really was a million dollars.

'It never happened and the rumours flew. One was that the demand would be so great they couldn't make them – hand laying of glass-fibre taking up a fair amount of space and they were awfully careful about curing the stuff for a long time. An alternative theory was that it would kill the E-type. Whether that's true or not I don't know. If they'd adjusted the profit margins correctly, they could have made an absolute killing, period, because it wasn't really using common components.

'Anyway it never happened, and Daimler faded. Of course, a lot of the machinery that was used to produce the V8 engine had First World War utility markings as well as Second World War. The line wasn't automated as such. Although the six-cylinder line was, by modern standards perhaps a bit crude, it did have a roller track and machine after machine in a logical sequence.

'With the Daimler it was – 25 cylinder heads, drill them, after lunch get a truck, barrow them down to another machine and do the next lot, type of thing! It would have needed some investment. Both the 450 and 250 engines would have needed investment in machinery to have gone further with them, and I suppose the variants of the six-cylinder made more sense.

———————

'We did the front end of the Mini Clubman. That was done at Jaguar.

'We did some Italian Mini designs. We only did some sketches and off they went on one of the Old Man's trips to Longbridge, when he was trying to justify how he fitted into the big corporation. He'd offered to assist with various things.

'Another we worked on was a Leyland gas turbine coach. We did some styling on that.

———————

'In the late sixties we had a BMW into the workshop and anybody under the age of 50 thought it was fantastic – it was the direction we ought to go.

'Everybody over the age of 50, who happened to have a bit of power, thought it was a horrible, tinny, German thing!'

———————

William Heynes recalls that he and Sayer came up with this design for a large saloon but that the 'Old Man' was not keen. (William Heynes)

In May 1979 the late Harry Mundy, then in charge of engine design and development at Jaguar, wrote to the late Claude Baily.

'Currently I have some V12 engines on 14:1 compression ratio, and operating quite satisfactorily on 4 star fuel. On a journey it is possible to achieve over 20 mpg as we are able to run on air fuel ratios of 18.5:1. This is achieved by using a very high turbulence chamber achieved by placing the exhaust valves of the V12 head in a recessed chamber somewhat similar to the old bath-tub design . . . .

'We are also developing a new range of light alloy 6 cylinder engines which will eventually replace both the XK and V12, because even with our improved combustion with the high compression heads, we shall still need to be able to meet the mandated 27 mpg consumption for America in 1985 with the latter.

Mundy went on to mention four valve heads. 'With a four valve 3.8 we can achieve 24-25 mpg. The first 3.8 version develops 237 bhp DIN – and these are true figures, not ------'s postulated figures.'

EIGHTIES

THE LATE HARRY MUNDY, former head of power unit design

Among senior engineering staff, there was considerable disagreement on the merits and demerits of the four-cam versus the two-cam V12 engine. It will be recalled that, with competition primarily in mind, the four-cam was the first to be designed and built. It was fitted in the unique XJ13 mid-engined sports racing car. Mundy belonged to the pro-two-cam camp and he was not known for mincing his words.

'The XJ13 was a complete waste of time and money. Installed in the car, the engine only gave about 480 horsepower. It gave 503, I think, with testbed exhausts.

'If the four cam engine, which I killed, had gone ahead in production, Jaguar wouldn't be in existence today.

'You couldn't get air pumps on it, power steering pumps – they were even going to the extent of designing an auxiliary power unit to go into the boot, to drive these things.

'It had a downdraught inlet port. These had been tried by BRM and Ferrari, and thrown away, and also on the Mercedes-Benz 300SLR, which barely gave 300 horsepower. This is because as the air comes in it always goes round the outside of the induction tracts. It went onto the cylinder wall, there was a restriction on air flow and on which the fuel separated out. That was the basic problem.

'As is well known, we also did a V8, as a single cam. It had a sort of tingling effect, a second-order resonance like a four-cylinder, which we could never really entirely get rid of. It also had unequal firing down each bank, but this was never criticised.

'We went to the May head on the V12 which enabled us to lengthen the stroke. We increased one to 6.4-litres and put it in a XJ12, which was a brilliant motor car. I could start off from Coventry in top gear and go to the middle of London in fifth gear. If I didn't have to stop, I never changed gear.

'It also had a five-speed gearbox which never went into production. They thought that Jaguars would all be automatic. If it had gone into production, the take-up of manuals would have been much more than 50 per cent, in my opinion, and would have made the XJ-S.

'I was responsible, despite what they may publish and tell you, for the new six-cylinder that is going in the XJ40 – entirely.'

JACKIE STEWART

'One of the great richnesses that Jaguar had was Sir William. He obviously had wonderful taste, because whoever was in there designing – and his team included Heynes and Lofty and all these people – at the end of the day, I think it all went down to Sir William, when it came to that style.

158

'The man was so unassuming and so mild. He always had his dark blue suit on, with his light blue tie and his white shirt. He was a wonderfully elegant man in himself, and almost an introvert within the industry.

'Yet he obviously had such a strong part to play. The SS100 was a fantastic looking car, I think, and then to produce the XK120 and follow it with the E-type – I think all of those cars were great.

'The present coupe car, the XJ-S, is neither hither or tither as far as I'm concerned. Funnily enough I drove one of the new saloons this morning and I thought I was in one of the old ones. I thought I was in an XJ6, not an XJ40. I felt as if I was looking over the car, rather than out of the car. It just didn't feel as if it was a modern car. It seems to have been left behind. The cosmetic changes that they made to it, which took such a long time to come around, really aren't so dramatic.

'On the other hand, the company's still alive. I just hope it can hold on, but I don't think it can hold on that long. At the moment there's a romance going on that might allow it to go, but for how long.

I mentioned to Stewart that the XJ40 was scheduled to last nine years.

'It's a long time. I wish them well. It's a wonderful name. If it takes something to keep it there, a relationship with somebody else to make sure it stays there, as long as the integrity remains, then I think fine.

'But Jaguar's certainly been one of the great ambassadors for the British motor industry.

Noted Jaguar restorer and enthusiast, Aubrey Finburgh, pedals his wares; or, perhaps it is a case of 'stop me and buy one'; or, perhaps, just his ideas on how to redesign his ancient van. The D-type front might well improve top speed and petrol consumption, but the complete XK120 front end can hardly help.

'The XK-SS was the Porsche 959 of its day. People would have paid any number of pounds, dollars or deutschmarks for one. That was something that I would have thought would really have gone – that people would have wanted to have.'

JACKIE STEWART

BILL JONES, who worked in the Body Shop and the Styling Department

'My brother Tom, who is 10 years older than me, brought me to Coventry. He'd been with Jaguar since 1940 and he came back to Wales for the Easter holiday in 1949. I was about to leave school and join a firm down there as a cabinet maker, but he said, "Do you want to come back and learn a trade in Coventry?"

'I think it was 1 May 1949 that I started. That was in Foleshill. Styling at Foleshill was a Nissen hut, with a dirt floor, and one of those old combustion stoves in the middle.

'The Experimental was on stilts. It had an old wooden floor. The knots would fall through and you could look down about 12 feet to the dirt that was below. In the body shop, in those days down there, everywhere they had a spot welding machine, they put a big sheet of steel down, so it wouldn't wear away.

ON FRED GARDNER:
'He was the Styling Department. You wouldn't need locks on the door with old Fred. All the high security we have today, he was the high security! You crossed him once, and you never went in there again.

'He ran the Wood Mill, because we had a lot of wood in the cars in the early days. I did nine months in there. He was half and half – wood mill and styling. There were no problems in the wood mill with Fred, no threat of a "downer" there. He was the Shop Steward as well as the gaffer, he always said that!

'At certain times, perhaps for a couple of hours, he'd come into the styling area. In there he had about ten body makers and four tinnies from Abbey Panels.

'Sir William always had the final decision on every styling detail.

'On every car we made, he spent more time on grilles than virtually the rest of the car. When you think about it it is the main feature of a car. When you look at them in a showroom, they are always pointing at you and that's the first impact. Even if it's turning a corner a hundred yards away, you know it's a Jaguar, because that's the Jaguar grille. We mustn't lose that.

'I made the XJ40 grille out of my head. We were down to three stylists. Everybody was frustrated. We were under Leyland. Leyland was killing it.

'Edwardes came and said, "Make it a Jaguar".

'Before that we'd had the Stokes's, and all the regimes. They'd all looked at it: "Best thing we've seen". But of course they'd been looking at Morris Marinas, all those sorts of things. "Oh well, we'll go up the Jag now and see what their turning out." That's what you felt they were doing, and I think anything would have pleased them. Regimes kept changing but we had to do something quickly because we wanted money off the Government. So we said, "For Christ's sake, let's put a grille on it".

'It was a fibre-glass car, and I made a wooden model, and a chap from Abbey Panels made the chrome grille, all the vanes in it. I had made grilles for Sir William, and he was missing at the time. Sir William had finished with us. It was in the latter two years of the XJ40 that he came back to put his little bit in it.

Gents and ladies both queued up to buy the stylish SS Jaguars which were offered with every convenience!

There are interesting parallels between the XK120, launched at the Motor Show in 1948, and the XJ220 Supercar, launched at the Motor Show forty years later.

Neither had even run before the Show. In spite of this, both 'stole' their respective Show though neither was intended as a production model.

In both instances the name was based on the 'estimated' top speed.

In its early tests, the XK120 only just exceeded the 100 mph mark.

To adjust a D-type clutch, you first have to remove the transmission tunnel and the picnic hamper. Bottoms up! (Philip Porter)

'As a kid, I'd seen blokes making grilles for him, and you'd think, "That's marvellous". You could look at that grille and look at that car, and it was straight dead on at the front – perfect. You'd go, say, 45 degrees and there was something wrong – it didn't look quite right.

'So you really had to cheat, and you'd say, "Right. Number four from centre line, pull it out a $^1/_{16}$. Eighth from centre line, push it in. It was all wrong if you did it on paper, but for looks it was perfect.

'Front head-on the grille would look good, but as you went round you'd think there was a kink in it. There wasn't. It was reflections and everything. We cheated to make it look good. Nobody else would know, but that's why a lot of time was always spent on the grille.

'There were even wire mesh grilles tried inside the mouth of the E-types before they were launched. Sir William always tried to set his grilles in a fraction. Even on the XJ6 it was in an aperture, just like the

Showing a slight contrast in size, the TWR Jaguar team transporter and the little motorised trolley for transporting wheels and tyres around the paddock.
(Jaguar Cars)

At Monza in 1988 TWR Jaguar established their supremacy over the Sauber Mercedes with Brundle and Cheever winning by more than a lap and the Jaguar moving into the Championship lead. (Jaguar Cars)

two headlamps, they were set in. In the early days they were on the outside, like the Bentley and the Rolls; he then went the other way. When he had two dummy horn grilles, they were set in a little aperture, which was beautiful coachwork.

'Nowadays we have a choice of, say, a dozen steering wheels. A steering wheel just came and he said that was the one we were having. Things were done so quickly then.

'But it was just the one person who mattered. It was Sir William's taste and his car, and everything rubbed off on all those old skilled blokes. When I went as a kid in 1949, many of them had been with him 20 years then. They were very elderly people who taught me my skills, but it was a pleasure.

BILL HEYNES talking of his late wife, Dutch.

'She used to drive my S.S.I, and once came back with both door handles missing!'

'Sir William always expected a high standard of work. But what is surprising, he spoke to very few people. He never spoke to his shop floor workers. If I was doing a job for him, he would call the Foreman. "Rogers. What's this man doing now?"

'He would never ask me if the job was going all right until his last years. When he came in the department, he recognised people who'd been loyal to him and stuck with him. There'd be somebody young in quite a responsible job but he wouldn't recognise him, so he'd come straight over.

'I remember towards the end of his life he'd had a fall. He was chauffered to Jaguar to look at something. So, obviously, he sat in the back. The Series III he came in had rise and fall seats, and sitting in the back, he could see the mechanism. He was out of that car – although he'd had a fall – called me and, oh, he went spare, as if it was my fault! Now, in his day, you would never see anything like that.

'I went to America on a styling clinic with the 40. The Americans just said, "You know what they want. They want class. They want British skill and British craftsmanship. If you want furniture, you want Chippendale. If you want nice china, you want Worcester. That's what they expect – keep it wood, keep it leather".

'I was ashamed to work here when it was under Leyland.

'We must keep it looking Jaguar, not follow these others. You can engineer them just the same, cause it's the looks of the car that matters. There's only a few of us left now.'

At the third attempt, in 1988, TWR raised the tally of Jaguar wins at Le Mans to six.

This medal was awarded by the State of California to the XK-E.
(Jaguar Cars)

Pat Smart, seen here centre, is today, the Chairman of the Jaguar Apprentices Association and Manager of Fleet Sales.

Miscellaneous weights

COOPER-JAGUAR
Total Weight: 2292 lb (20 cwt 1 qtr 24 lb)
Weight distribution: 50.6/49.4
MARK VII WITH LIGHT ALLOY BODY – KRW 621
Total weight: 29 cwt 3 qtr 23 lb
Spare wheel, tool kit, lightweight bucket seats.
PRODUCTION MARK VII
Total weight: 34 cwt 1 qtr 26 lb
LAGONDA 2.9-LITRE
Total weight: 32^1/4 cwt
XK120D
Total dry weight: 17 cwt 3 qtr 16 lb
Complete with full racing equipment.
PRODUCTION XK140 WITH BORG-WARNER FITTED
Total weight: 28 cwt 2 qtr 0 lb
Full tank.
MERCEDES-BENZ 300SL
Total weight: 25^1/2 cwt
With tool kit, spare wheel, 13 gals of fuel. Scale weight
LISTER-JAGUAR
Total weight: 17 cwt 3 qtr 0 lb

TOM JONES, who played a leading role on creating most of the competition and production Jaguars until his retirement in 1985

'I joined Jaguar in 1940, and did 45 years with the company. I firstly did two weeks in the shop as an electrician's mate, straight from college, and within two weeks they felt that I could read a drawing and I was asked if I wanted a job in the Drawing Office.

'So I then went on to jigs and tools for two and a half years. The war was still on and I got seconded to work with Claude Baily, doing the forerunners of the XK engine, the folding sidecar and the jeep thing that we were going to do.

'During the latter part of the war, we were working in a shed out the back doing these odd Ministry jobs. When the war finished I worked on engines and gearboxes. Then I took on automatic transmissions and I was responsible for their installation in all Jaguars.

'At that time they brought in a man by the name of Albert Moore and split Claude Baily's job of Chief Designer job into Engines and Transmissions, and Chassis. Bill Thornton was in charge of bodies at the time. I was put to work with Albert Moore on chassis as the Assistant Chief Designer. He lasted 10 months and then they gave me the job!

'I had something to do with the C-type, therefore, and from '53 on I was responsible to Bill Heynes for all the competition models.

'Sir William very rarely came into the Drawing Office, but one day he came in when we were doing the XJ6 and Bob Knight and I put some facts before him on where we could take some Mercedes sales.

'He said, "Do you think we could sell a thousand a week? If we can, we'll go for one car".

'That's why the big saloon was eventually dropped. He didn't want to do another big saloon and when it got down to 50 a week, it was hardly viable.'

When we chatted in 1985, I asked Tom if there had been any thoughts of a Mark II replacement.

'It's been thought of recently, in the last three years. When the XJ6 was launched, it had a 109-inch wheelbase, and then for the long wheelbase version, we stretched it four inches. That was really to get sufficient room inside. It was really felt that that was the minimum occupant size that we could really have for a Jaguar.

'A lot of people think that we could have made a small saloon, but I don't think we could keep the Jaguar standards, the refinement, and remain competitive pricewise. This is what we came up with three years ago. It was felt we could do with a smaller car because we'd lost what we call the "executive market" in this country. The price was too high and we'd lost the market to cars like the Ford Granada.

'We did an exercise using XJ40 components, obviously for cost reasons, but unfortunately weight and costwise, it wasn't on. So it does mean that if they ever do one, it will have to be a brand new car again. I think the right thing for Jaguar is to go up market rather than down market from the 40.

The XJ220 stole the 1988 Motor Show in a way that was reminiscent of that Lyons masterpiece of exactly 40 years earlier – the XK120 Super Sports. (Jaguar Cars)

To say that the XJ220 interior moved away from the Jaguar tradition would be something of an understatement. No picnic tables here! (Jaguar Cars)

For a number of years, there seemed to be a gap in the market for a company to do for Jaguar what Alpina had done for BMW. Eventually that void was filled, appropriately, by TWR. (Philip Porter)

'I had to stop the new XJ41 sports car two years ago and put it on one side. I felt that if we didn't, we wouldn't achieve the 40 programme, which we were losing ground on.

———

'Aluminium was considered for the E-type. We had done the first 240 XK120s in aluminium before switching over to steel, and that was in everybody's mind. It is all right for competition cars, and it is still thought about for production cars. You go through it every so often.

'We started off thinking about it for the XJ40 to get the weight out. We considered bolt-on panels in aluminium, but I think what killed that in the end was that the capital expenditure went from £56m to £94m if we used aluminium panels.

'You have to heat treat the panels and you have to press them within three days. So the only way to do it, really, is to have furnaces alongside the press shop. You have to anneal the panels to keep them soft, so it was like a continuous process which meant installing all these furnaces.

'So that was out because we only had £100m to do the whole car, and you couldn't spend it just on the body!

———

'The E-type was not really ready by the time of the launch. I don't know whether it was a deliberate policy, but Sir William never built a car unless it was sold.

'It was the same thing with the XJ6. There were hardly any cars for months after it was launched. Some drawings were not released till after the launch! He'd change his mind about things, and the other thing was that he got opinions at the launch, and then he would rush this in, rush that in. He didn't wait till next year's model!

'There was one man he always brought in before a launch for his opinion, and that was old man Henly himself. Of course his wife was the other one, who really had a say. We had to ship the cars out to Wappenbury and she had a look. I think he took a lot of notice of his wife.'

List of XJ Numbers

(XJ = experimental Jaguar – applied to projects. Those missing may not have been assigned.)

XJ3	S-type Saloon
XJ4	XJ6 Saloon
XJ5	4.2 Litre Mark X
XJ8	E-type 2 + 2
XJ10	XJ12 Saloon
XJ13	Mid-engined Sports Racing Car
XJ16	420 Saloon
XJ17	Series II E-type 2 + 2
XJ21	Possible E-type replacement
XJ22	Series II E-type
XJ23	Initially intended to be 'E-type Stage 2 facelift with V12 engine', then probably SII
XJ24	Not assigned according to Jaguar
XJ25	Series III E-type V12 2 + 2
XJ26	Series III E-type V12 Open
XJ27	XJ-S V12 Coupe
XJ28	XJ-S V12 Cabriolet
XJ29	Series I XJ6 LWB Saloon
XJ30	Series I XJ12 LWB Saloon
XJ31	Series II XJ6 LWB Saloon

XJ32	Series II XJ12 LWB Saloon	
XJ32	Series II XJ12	
XJ33	Probably – Series I XJ6 2 Door Coupe	
XJ34	Probably – Series I XJ12 2 Door Coupe	
XJ35	Series II XJ6 2 Door Coupe	
XJ36	Series II XJ12 2 Door Coupe	
XJ37	Series II XJ6 2 Door Coupe (may be 3.4, though not produced)	
XJ40	XJ6 Saloon	
XJ41	New Sports Car	
XJ43	Series II 4.2 Vanden Plas Saloon	

XJ50	Series III V12 Saloon
XJ51	Series III 3.4 Saloon
XJ52	Series III 4.2 Saloon
XJ53	Series III 4.2 Vanden Plas Saloon
XJ54	Series III V12 Vanden Plas Saloon
XJ57	XJS 6 Cyl Coupe
XJ58	XJS 6 Cyl Cabriolet
XJ59	Series III Diesel Saloon
XJ60	Series III converted to XJ40 front and rear suspension
XJ77	XJS V12 Convertible
XJ82	LWB XJ40 with V12 engine
XDM/1	Daimler $2^1/2$ V8 engined

	Mark I saloon *
XDM/2	Daimler $2^1/2$ V8 engined Mark II saloon *
XDM/3	Daimler Limousine
XDM/62	Daimler Limousine – Middle East Specification
XDM/65	Daimler Limousine – USA Specification

*This is my theory! Certainly XDM/1 was a Daimler engined Mark I or II. The engine was first put in a Mark I but I can find no reference to XDM/2 and thus I think it is reasonably safe to assume the above. *P.P.*
